Evaluating the Personnel Function

Shaun Tyson and Alan Fell

Hutchinson

London   Melbourne   Sydney   Auckland   Johannesburg

Hutchinson Education

An imprint of Century Hutchinson Limited
Brookmount House, 62-65 Chandos Place,
London WC2N 4NW

Century Hutchinson Australia Pty Ltd
PO Box 496, 16-22 Church Street, Hawthorn, Victoria 3122, Australia

Century Hutchinson New Zealand Limited
32-34 View Road, PO Box 40-086, Glenfield, Auckland 10, New Zealand

Century Hutchinson South Africa (Pty) Limited
PO Box 337, Bergvlei 2012, South Africa

First published 1986
Reprinted 1987, 1988

© Shaun Tyson and Alan Fell 1986

Set in VIP Century Schoolbook by
Colset Pte Ltd, Singapore

Printed and bound in Great Britain by
Anchor Brendon Limited, Tiptree, Essex

British Library Cataloguing in Publication Data
Tyson, Shaun
  Evaluating the personnel function. – (Hutchinson
  personnel management series)
  1. Personnel management
  I. Title   II. Fell, Alan
  658.3   HF5549

ISBN 0 09 164151 9

Contents

Acknowledgements

We have drawn on many sources when preparing this critique of personnel management. In addition to the published works, to which we refer in the text, we have been fortunate in receiving stimulating and helpful comments from a number of company chairmen and chief executives who responded to our enquiries. We were also granted the opportunity to try out our arguments and ideas at three seminars held at Brunel University and two at the Irish Management Institute, with practising personnel managers, on middle and senior management programmes run at Cranfield School of Management, and with personnel students at the London School of Economics: a total of over two hundred people. We gained many insights from these discussions which we have incorporated within the book. We owe a particular debt of gratitude to David Guest for his detailed comments on an earlier draft.

We are grateful for permission to reproduce the table on 'Typology of Evaluations' which originally appeared in the '*Strategy of Evaluation Research*' by Dr P. Hesseling published by Van Gorcum & Company. Finally, we wish to thank June Wardill, Sue Brookes and Dorothy Rogers for typing the manuscript so enthusiastically, and so well.

Shaun Tyson
Alan Fell
May 1985

Dedicated by Alan Fell to the memory of his father, in final vindication; and to his mother and Ruth as some reward for their forbearance.

1
The Crisis in Personnel Management

This book is about the way specialists in personnel management perform their role. All managers of people are 'personnel managers' in the literal sense, that is they have a personnel function to perform. Our concern is with the role performed by those who specialize in the personnel function; whose purpose is to propose, coordinate and implement agreed policies in such areas as industrial relations, reward structures, management development, training, recruitment and promotion, redundancy, redeployment and on the conditions of service. They are thus the specialists in managing the employment relationship.

How to manage people at work successfully has been a major question since industrialization began. One answer to this question by senior managers with a direct accountability for people and their work has been to appoint specialists in the employment relationship, whose role is supportive of this task. Such specialized personnel staff are now to be found throughout the world, in commerce, industry and government organizations, with remits which range from total personnel responsibility to sub-specialisms in training, compensation, manpower planning and welfare for example. Not only are there many different job titles (Human Resource Director, Personnel Manager, Men's Employment Manager, Training Manager, Welfare Officer, Compensation Adviser to name but a few), but these occupations are performed in differing ways, in a variety of organization structures.

Given that the appointment of these specialists is one answer to the question of how to manage people, how effective an answer is it? Up to the mid 1970s, the growth and spread of specialist personnel managers indicated that for many organizations the formalization of the personnel role, especially in respect of industrial relations, and its separation from line management was an essential ingredient for modern management. The principles of the division of labour have resulted in the creation of a range of specialized functionaries, so personnel management was developed as part of that trend. On the whole, there was evidence that the appointment of personnel specialists was an acceptable answer to the question for senior managers; proving how effective an answer is another matter.

This would seem to be an opportune moment for a critique of personnel management in the United Kingdom. The structural changes to the staple industries, with attendant unemployment are part of a major recession in which the roles of all managerial functions are being questioned. Personnel management was established as a specialism at a time of high employment, as part of an expansionary trend. The onset of the recession has raised fundamental questions about its value. Our purpose in preparing this critique is to establish the ways in which personnel specialists can contribute to their employers' businesses. This entails providing the thinking practitioner with ways in which to evaluate the personnel function of management. The book is divided into two parts. Chapters 1 to 4 give a critique of the specialist personnel function where we are expanding on what we believe the role of personnel management to be. Chapters 5 to 8 are a discussion of the measures which may be used to evaluate personnel work.

There have been periodic crises of confidence among personnel practitioners, a cause of comment among management writers, where the value of personnel management as a specialism has been questioned.[1] The main charge is that personnel specialists have failed to live up to their own claims as 'professionals'. They have been unable to solve problems of managing people, and have failed to gain the necessary authority for success in their role.[2]

Given that personnel specialists lack direct accountability for employees, and the lateral sources of their authority, these charges may be unfair, but they stick.[3] After all, if the response of personnel managers is that they lack authority, this could be interpreted as a sign of weakness, or of inability to gain the confidence of top management, and this leads to the next question – do we need personnel managers at all? Even if Townsend's advice, given in *Up the Organization*, to fire the personnel manager is not followed, the vulnerability of the personnel specialists' role has been established.[4]

The major recession which has affected Western Europe and the USA since the late 1970s has produced new difficulties for personnel management. There are twin crises, one internal, the other external to the occupation. There is a crisis in confidence among personnel managers themselves, and a related crisis over their credibility among their managerial colleagues. Evidence of a new found uncertainty can be discovered in the pages of management journals, where articles seeking to justify the relevance of specialist personnel management work have become increasingly common. The following comments give an impression of the crisis:

failure to understand the function has led to the appointment of amateurs, or failures, to a task which requires considerable analytical and personal skills.[5]

a practising personnel director has written that 'at present a kind of generalized inferiority complex pervades the personnel field'.[6]

In many companies, personnel departments face growing disenchantment, and a steady decline in their influence.[7]

little agreement exists on what Human Resource Management is or what it should be.[8]

Personnel has constantly to establish its credibility before being able to contribute. . .[9]

Personnel management in the UK has failed to generate or be associated with, an overall set of social, political and economic objectives which are acceptable to the major economic decision makers.[10]

There has even been a questioning, in the light of cost cutting exercises of the very role of personnel management, particularly in the public sector.[11]

The run down of manufacturing, with consequential structural unemployment, raises the question: what contribution can personnel managers make? It is difficult for personnel staff to see how they can solve people problems at the enterprise level, when the industry in which they work is driven by economic forces to a point where the survival of the business is at stake. Pressure on 'overheads' and on personnel departments, already defined by some senior managers as extras to the business, has reduced the growth of the personnel specialism.

Year on year increases in membership of the Institute of Personnel Management (IPM) were as high as 14% in 1968 and 1969, rising to 15% in 1970, and 16% in 1971. The rate of increase then steadied to around 5% per annum until 1977, when membership fell to 18,106 from 18,554 in 1976. Membership of the Institute in 1984 was 23,332. This includes 5000 students and 3400 affiliates. Membership had only grown by 1500 people in the previous four years.[12] The 1982 report of the Advisory, Conciliation and Arbitration service warned that:

> The decline in the numbers and in the influence of personnel managers has gone a little beyond what might simply have been expected from the impact of the recession, and reversed a trend that had been a notable feature of industrial relations in the previous decade.
>
> This may be partly a result of cost-cutting falling hardest on support services during a period of recession. It is also part of a much more general change in philosophy to return as much responsibility for management as possible to the line manager and in particular to the first line supervisor, while wider issues are passed to a higher level with the intermediate grades of personnel management cut out.[13]

In the public sector, the Cassels Report on personnel work in the Civil Service sought to show the advantages of devolving the activities of personnel management to government departments, as a move away from the control and operation of personnel policy in a central unit in such areas as recruitment, appraisal and career management. The central Management and Personnel Office is to retain responsibilities for senior staff development, and will act as an auditor of local departmental personnel functions. At the local level: 'each department should develop a coherent personnel strategy, tailored to its needs'.[14]

There has also been a change in the attitudes of governments towards working people. The policies of the Reagan administration in the USA, and of the Thatcher government in the UK embody a laissez-faire ideology, the credo of which is competition, individualism and the survival of the fittest. By contrast, personnel policies typically have been founded on the provision of welfare benefits, on principles of fairness and standardization of treatment for specific groups, and have often derived their force from the collective bargains which sustain these principles. Treating people as aggregates runs counter to this re-asserted Western tradition of individualism. Kierkegaard expresses this distaste for seeing people as members of a collectivity:

> In his conscience and in his responsibility before God, i.e. through his consciousness of being eternal, everyone is an individual. A mass he never becomes, nor lost in a 'public'. His responsibility towards eternity saves him from that which characterizes the animals, namely that they are a crowd, a mass, a public or whatever other impulse it is which causes one to have to speak of human beings as if one were speaking of a drove of oxen.[15]

The bureaucratization of work, with formal rules to govern selection, promotion, discipline, etc., lends itself to the representation of employee interests by trade unions,[16] and it has been argued that the need for personnel and industrial relations specialists is directly related to the growth of collective bargaining at the company, or plant level.[17] The movement towards an individualistic philosophy could therefore be seen as a contradiction of the need for personnel specialists. If individuals can negotiate their pay, promotion and other similar matters directly with their own managers, what role is there for personnel managers? Personnel managers have often seemed to their line manager colleagues to be the 'no sayers', the guardians of pay scales, of procedures, and conformity. With trade unions on the defensive, a plentiful supply of labour, and the new ideology, who needs personnel managers?

One of the chief reasons for writing this book is our belief that personnel managers need to rethink their role, to overcome the difficulties inherent in their position. The recession has both threatened those with personnel responsibilities and provided an opportunity for the personnel specialist to help the organization adapt to change. There is a new industrial relations game to be played. The old rules are no longer valid. For personnel managers to take advantage of the opportunities provided by the recession, they will have to show how they can play the game by the new rules. These new 'rules' include more direct contact with the workforce, through parallel communication channels to those with the unions, more employee involvement, greater flexibility in response to market conditions, better control of employee costs, better use of information technology, and the creation of more effective management teams.

Our analysis is thus at the level of the organization, and we address the problems of personnel management in the hope that we will provide insights for the serious student of managerial arts, whether they are experienced practitioners, or are facing these problems for the first time. It is our intention also to engage the interest of those line managers who interact with personnel specialists, so that they may come to understand the value of the personnel role, and will be able to make a realistic assessment of its contribution to their businesses.

We will not be offering a simple prescription. Our refusal to offer the blandishments of a miracle cure for all economic ills stems from our vision of the problems themselves. The problems of management are no more or less than the problems of existence. The psychological predicament of which one's working life is a part, defies simple solutions or ready-made techniques based on some unifying principle; the meaning of life and the value of personal identity require discussion of a philosophical and religious nature. Nevertheless, personnel managers encounter these deep areas of personal existence by their concern with employment relationships. Issues such as the distribution of income in society, the threat to personal identity caused by redundancy and the way that power over employees is exercised are all of significance for personnel managers. In the chapters that follow, we will concentrate on the more 'practical' issues of everyday managerial life. In doing so, however, we are conscious of the deeper paradoxes from which these practical affairs evolve.

Most personnel specialists have been trained at a time of full employment. The high activity rates in post-war Britain now seem an aberration. The combination of a major recession in world trade, the emergence of new manufacturing nations, the disappearance of old skills and crafts, the rise in white-collar jobs, and unsympathetic legislation is forcing trade unions towards institutional changes. The unspoken question for many people now is has our economic decline actually gone so far that it is irreversible? With the UK becoming a net importer of manufactured goods (including the new technologies where import penetration in electronic computers reached 90% in 1979) in 1983 for the first time in recent history, and the continued rise in unemployment, deindustrialization, the 'North – South divide' and more people, especially women, seeking work, the problems faced by the UK are clearly not just to do with our industrial relations, but reflect endemic problems of a society in transition.

Simplistic explanations of our economic and social difficulties have frequently been offered by the popular press to the effect that trade unions have caused rigidities in the labour market, have had a ratchet effect on wages, and have inhibited change.[18] According to this vision, our troubles stem from 'weak' management, and a failure to 'stand up' to the unions. Even if one accepts that in some cases this may have been true in the 1960s and early 1970s, there are other reasons that could be advanced including the mismanagement of the economy by successive governments, inadequate investment, failures to adapt new technologies quickly enough, badly educated managers, and badly educated working people,[19] as well as political issues such as defence expenditure beyond our capacity to pay and our European Community commitments.

There is no real evidence that our pay is excessive, indeed there is an enormous amount of poverty in the UK, with millions of people eligible for supplementary benefits.[20] Strike statistics are difficult to compare internationally, but again it would seem that the UK record is better than many other industrialized countries, such as Australia, Italy and France.[21] There are many examples of successful attempts to restructure relationships with the trade unions, such as at British Leyland, Vickers and British Airways. Less success has been achieved in the strongly unionized environments of the mining and steel industries. It could be argued that an industrial relations system is a way of acting out conflicts in a ritual fashion. This keeps the fabric of our society intact and allows us to maintain the democratic basis for action. Although conflict may limit the possibilities for rapid change, it does allow our citizens a degree of freedom, and a relatively comfortable life for the majority. Our society has already shown its flexibility since it has had to adapt to many changes such as the continuing concentration of British business, multi-racialism, and periods of high inflation.

The expertise used to control the employment relationship, which means exacting effort in the production process places personnel specialists at the centre of these issues. The quality and quantity of work are now high on the agenda of management. The methods and systems for developing a high volume, and a high quality output are thus important. In many companies, the emphasis has now shifted from maintaining harmony in industrial relations towards output goals. Major concerns for personnel managers here are individual performance standards, selection tests for appropriate qualities and skills in the employee, training, in job-related skills and in customer relationships, management development, better communications, the reassertion of a leadership role for first-line supervisors, more management team building, and value for money in personnel policies. This heralds a shift towards 'employee' relations rather than industrial relations. A move, in fact, to an individualistic rather than a collective ideology.

The management of employee relations is typically a pragmatic affair, where actions are taken in accordance with a philosophy of management derived from the particular circumstances of the organization, and the ideology of the managers and workpeople. The evidence we have is that managers of industrial relations in Britain, with their long voluntarist tradition, have usually made ad hoc responses to conflict, and have been 'satisficers', looking for the solution which works, rather than a 'best' solution in any absolute sense. To adapt the old adage, managers in this tradition are not looking for the sharpest needle in the haystack, but rather for a needle sharp enough to sew with. Informal agreements and procedures abound, since managers prefer freedom of action in day-to-day decision-making within the overall guidance of their Board of Directors.[22] If the state and trade unions are unwilling or unable to protect individual interests, we might expect a resurgence of company policies to fill the vacuum. As more attention is given to local bargaining, and to local initiatives in communications, so enterprise unions may become the norm. Already Japanese companies operating in the UK have shown that it is possible to adopt a radical approach. Single status organizations, with one trade union, pendulum arbitration, long-term agreements, quality circles, and a disciplined workforce are some elements of a new British industrial relations.

We have been making generalizations. There may, however, be industries emerging – the sunrise industries – in which individuals develop their own career, and negotiate individually their reward packages. The bulk of personnel work is still conducted in organizations where the sun seems to be at its zenith; some of these organizations, although relatively stable (such as the Health Service, British Rail, and large oil companies) are changing to meet new pressures and demands. In others, small factories, or jobbing engineering works, there may be a hand to mouth existence, where the future is dependent on the next order. For a vast number of offices, shops, and small companies there is a routine personnel administration function, where change is not reflected in its everyday purpose. In the pages that follow, we will address a number of questions that stem from the current state of personnel management. Three main issues emerge. What kind of personnel function will best meet the needs of our corporations now and in the future? What personnel policies should we pursue? How can we best evaluate the achievement of the personnel function of management? In Chapter 2 we describe different types of personnel function, as a necessary first step in our analysis.

Notes

1 G. Hunter, *The Role of the Personnel Officer* (London: IPM, 1957).
  G. Ritzer and H. Trice, *An occupation in conflict: A study of the personnel manager* (New York: Cornell University, 1969).
  K. Legge, *Power, Innovation and Problem-solving in Personnel Management* (London: McGraw-Hill, 1978).
  T.J. Watson, *The Personnel Managers* (London: Routledge and Kegan Paul, 1977).
  S. Tyson, *Specialists in Ambiguity: Personnel Management as an Occupation* (PhD Thesis: London University, 1979).
2 Royal Commission on Trade Unions and Employers' Associations 1965–1968, *Donovan Report*, Cmnd 3623 (London: HMSO, 1968).
  K. Legge and M. Exley, 'Authority, ambiguity and adaptation: the personnel specialist's dilemma', *Industrial Relations Journal*, vol. 6, no. 3 (1975), pp. 51–65.
3 E. Gross, 'Sources of lateral authority in personnel departments', *Industrial Relations*, vol. 3 (1964), pp. 121–133.
4 R. Townsend, *Up the Organization* (London: Michael Joseph, 1970).
5 J. Henstridge, 'Personnel management – a framework for analysis', *Personnel Review*, vol. 4, no. 1 (1975), p. 51.

6 Legge and Exley, 'Authority, ambiguity and adaptation', p. 51.
7 K. Manning, 'The rise and fall of personnel', *Management Today* (March 1983), p. 74.
8 J.D. Ross, 'A definition of human resource management', *Personnel Journal* (October 1981), p. 781.
9 P. Copping and C. Pickles, 'Who goes into Personnel?', *Personnel Executive* (October 1981), p. 31.
10 K. Thurley, 'Personnel management in the UK – a case for urgent treatment?', *Personnel Management* (August 1981), p. 28.
11 D. Guest, 'Has the recession really hit personnel management?', *Personnel Management* (October 1982), p. 36.
12 IPM *Annual Reports*.
See also 'A strategy for developing the Institute', *IPM Digest* (December 1984).
13 *ACAS Report* (London: HMSO, 1982).
14 J.S. Cassels, Management and Personnel Office, *Review of Personnel Work in the Civil Service. Report to the Prime Minister* (HMSO, 1983), p. 48.
15 J. Hohlenberg, *Soren Kierkegaard* (London: 1954), pp. 189–190.
16 G.S. Bain, *The Growth of White Collar Unionism* (Oxford: Clarendon Press, 1970).
B. Daniel, 'Who handles personnel issues in British industry?', *Personnel Management* (December 1983).
17 H.A. Turner, G. Roberts and D. Roberts, *Management characteristics and labour conflict* (Cambridge: Cambridge University Press, 1977).
18 'Stoppages caused by industrial disputes in 1983', *Employment Gazette* (July 1984), p. 308.
B. Burdetsky and H.S. Katzman, 'Is the strike iron still hot?', *Personnel Journal (July 1984)*.
19 *Final Report of Education Policy Panel of BIM under chairmanship of Brian Wolfson* (July 1982).
G. Crocker and P. Elias, 'British managers: a study of their education, training, mobility and earnings' *British Journal of Industrial Relations* vol. XXll, no. 1 March 1984.
20 'EEC long term unemployment proposals', *European Industrial Relations Review*, no. 130 (November 1984).
21 'International comparison of stoppages', *Employment Gazette* (March 1984), p. 101.
22 A. Marsh, *Industrial Relations Policy and Decision Making* (Aldershot: Gower, 1982).

2
Models of Personnel Management

The organizational and cultural context of personnel work

In this chapter we will set out the main approaches to personnel management in the United Kingdom. We will argue that to understand behaviour in organizations account has to be taken of the strategies pursued by organization members and that we should study both the actions managers take and the consequences. This is consistent with the contingency theory of organizations.

Action in organizations is contingent on the history, the technology in use, the values and beliefs of the actors on the organizational stage, and in particular upon their definitions of the situation.[1] All of these factors are conditioned by a range of broader issues, especially the economic position of the organization and government policies towards the economy and employment.

One of the chief variables that we might expect to determine the kind of personnel function in an organization is the state of development of the organization. For example, in a new company, on a 'green fields' site, we might expect the major interest to be in recruitment, training and organization design. Only later, when the company grows and changes would we anticipate more sophisticated manpower planning and employee relations policies to be introduced. The trouble is, this does not tell us *how* the personnel job is done, but merely gives an indication of the activities in which managers are employed. Thus, the kind of consultancy service offered by a highly experienced personnel manager to the new entrepreneurs on the 'green fields' site might be equally successful if offered to the top executive of an ageing nationalized industry, who is about to embark on a large redundancy programme.

In the management of people, how the task is completed is as important as which task is completed.[2] Within the personnel management canon there is room for many different approaches or ways of acting. From the research completed so far in this field it would appear that personnel managers are 'organization men' par excellence.[3] Their organizational orientation is a central part of their occupational ideology. Because personnel management seems to be about the organization itself, any kind of generalization is difficult. The type of personnel department is both a product of the organization's culture, and helps to create that culture.

An organization's culture seems to derive from a whole range of variables – the numbers employed, the industrial relations history, the level of trust exhibited between work people and management, and the geographical dispersion of employing units for example.[4] Certain styles of behaving are thought to be appropriate in accordance with the norms of behaviour which have developed, and with which newcomers are socialized. Personnel managers, from say the HQ of ICI, Shell International and the British Civil Service, would probably find themselves able to operate with only a minimum induction period in each other's job. The main difficulty would be for the more specialized personnel manager moving into the Civil Service, where specialization in personnel is only just being tried out. Even so, the hierarchical structure, rule-bound environment, large numbers and sophisticated decision-making rituals would soon make each transplant feel at home. By contrast, for any of the above to swop places with a personnel officer in a small jobbing engineering works would induce a severe culture shock.

We can accept that the organization culture is a forum where personnel management can be conducted within the established norms. But, again, a knowledge of the culture does not tell us *how* the personnel manager performs his work. Cultures are changed by new personnel policies and, therefore, the personnel manager cannot be merely a creature of the local organization culture.

Let us take the case of a division of a large US multinational operating in the UK, where changes in the design of nuclear power stations and falling demand for products used in the manufacture of steel were only foreseen a year in advance. There were no new products developed to replace the dying markets. Managers who had typically 20–30 years' service found that following the necessary redundancies a whole new environment was created, where new roles and relationships had to be developed, where the reward and promotion structures were more 'realistic' and where they were no longer insulated from the uncertainties of business. The personnel director and the MD provided a major change programme through training and new policies which set the company on a new course.

What seems to be significant in this example is that the approach taken by those with responsibility for the personnel function – the managing director and the personnel director – was to use the personnel function in the creation of a new culture and, one could say, a new company. It is, therefore, not just a matter of difference between industries or between industrial relations systems which creates distinct approaches to personnel management.

The central value system of the organization is expressed through its personnel policies. The organization's stability and capacity to survive are the mainspring of its culture, and are reflected in its business policy. For example, the marketing approach, the public relations, the corporate image and customer relationships of companies such as IBM or Marks and Spencer have a coherence. We would argue that how their recruitment, socialization, training, appraisal, promotion, reward and employee relations policies are conducted is a major contribution to the culture.

The frame of symbolic ideas and values with which personnel specialists engage employees is a way of legitimating the organization culture. The practices of differentiation between groups are institutionalized by symbols, such as the 'staff restaurant', the 'company car', and even the regulated physical distance between directors, managers and workpeople are sustained through customs, traditions and personnel policies which represent what those in control of the company believe about the way people should relate at work.

The culture of a people, whether within an organization or not, develops from their history. We will begin our search for the current models of personnel work in the United Kingdom by providing an account of the traditions in personnel management. The historical development of the role in the United Kingdom may be described by examining the significant events, and the typical ways of acting which have emerged in what may be called distinct 'traditions'.

Interpretation of the everyday world must of necessity be in language, and ideas, which stand together in clusters of meaning. These meanings become important as traditions when they are handed on, in stories, at conferences, by the media, in training, through books and in articles as part of the occupation's identity. For example, the ideas behind the concept of joint consultation seem to have become influential as a preferred style of managing, which we may attribute to the training of personnel managers.[5] Traditions, customs and 'folklore' are no doubt important in sustaining an organization's culture. A personnel manager from Bryant and May, the match manufacturers, described in 1970, to one of the authors, how the match girls' strike of 1888 was still 'remembered' as part of the industrial relations folklore of the company.

Another example is the attempt by certain occupational groups, such as railway engine drivers and printers, to maintain craft status, high earnings and a separate identity long after new technology has 'deskilled' their work. Managements also seem bound by organizational traditions. This was illustrated by the decision-making habits of the managing director of a large chain of shops in the mid 1960s where one of the authors was personnel manager. The managing director still thought about financial reporting as he had done when there were only two shops, one of which he managed, although his empire had grown to over 400 outlets and 4000 people. He could never reconcile himself to the growth, and still insisted on knowing what the week's takings were every Friday evening!

The history of each company, the markets in which it operates, the industrial relations traditions under which it has grown and the ventures it attempts help to distinguish the way in which specialist personnel management has developed. The main traditions in personnel management have produced expectations about the occupation – expectations which have led personnel managers to act in what they have come to regard as their best interest. We may, therefore, discover in these traditions of personnel, the origins of current models of personnel management.

The welfare tradition

The early specialists in the employment relationship were primarily concerned with the welfare of individual workers. In the 1890s, these early welfare workers often operated on an extramural basis and were mostly involved with the welfare of women working for the more enlightened employers. As part of the industrial betterment movement, welfare workers played their part in modernizing attitudes towards work people and, especially in the Quaker companies, attempted to demonstrate that the search for profit was not necessarily at the expense of the individual worker.[6]

The welfare tradition is still deeply embedded in the personnel function of many organizations. From this tradition comes the notion of personnel work being conducted from outside the main concerns of the business, and with different objectives. Welfare workers were often critics of management, and sometimes regarded individual employees as their clients. From this tradition comes the vision of personnel management as a 'loyal opposition' representing an alternative view to that of management.[7] In helping individuals, the personnel function becomes enmeshed in the everyday personal concerns of the workpeople, for their own sake, rather than because of any business motive. It has been argued that welfare work in this way helped to make capitalism acceptable, and we might say that even if it is unintended, one of the latent functions of the welfare tradition is to induce a reciprocal sense of obligation in the employee in response to the company's welfare actions.[8] As a further extension of this thesis, welfare work could be seen as a part of a management strategy to keep out trade unions, or to undermine their benefits. Such a fear was openly expressed by trade unions in the early 1920s.[9] However, we would distinguish between the latent function of welfare work, and an explicit strategy for trade union avoidance. This latter strand belongs more to the industrial relations tradition, than to the welfare tradition.

The industrial relations tradition

Industrial relations has traditionally been the province of the line manager, and of the officials and advisers from the employers' associations. Originally, these advisers often worked with a counterpart in the company, and most companies kept records of disputes, days lost and grievances handled, such as those required by the procedure agreement of the Engineering Employers' Federation.[10] One of the chief characteristics of British industrial relations is the voluntary nature of the agreements, and until recently there was no state intervention in collective relationships. There is still reliance upon tacit understandings at the plant, or workplace level, where the role of shop stewards has grown as negotiations have moved away from the national level.

The tight labour markets experienced in the 1960s and early 1970s put pressure on employers to grant high pay settlements to militant trade unions, and with a high level of aggregate demand it was easier to give in and raise prices, than to fight the unions over pay. The problems of incomes policies, and public service disputes (such as the 'winter of discontent' in 1979) enhanced the attention paid to industrial relations. Although there is little hard evidence, public opinion, as expressed through the media, came to regard poor industrial relations as one of the main causes of British lack of competitiveness. This was exemplified by the attention given to strikes in the ailing motor industry and demarcation disputes in shipbuilding. The British approach to industrial relations to date has demonstrated that procedures and systems work well in stable, traditional industries, until a major change is proposed. They can then have the effect of sustaining resistance to change. The 'fire fighting', ad hoc approaches adopted by line managers and personnel specialists towards industrial relations seem likely to produce sub-optimal decisions, which reduce operational efficiency in the long run.[11]

In a number of case studies comparing British and German manpower and industrial relations strategies, it was noted that German managements regard stability of employment as a conscious objective, and maintain internal labour markets in a stable state by restricting job opportunities. They achieve this by being more flexible in manpower utilization with a cooperative union movement. By contrast British management tends to dismiss workers, and hire them as needed thus transferring the costs to the community. The adversarial form of industrial relations which emerges 'has tended to inculcate a more acute sense of anxiety towards change among British workers. In the absence of multi-unionism, institutional conflicts within the enterprise do not arise [in Germany], as they do among competing unions in Britain'.[12]

British industrial relations specialists have therefore tended until recently to maintain the status quo, resisted change and have regarded institutional arrangements as inviolate, irrespective of the needs of the business.

The manpower control tradition

Personnel departments seem to have been established in response to the growth in numbers of people employed in organizations, to the complexity of the business, and as a response to a felt need for the formalization of procedures in people management. Examples of this can be seen in the histories of ICI, Courtaulds, and Marks and Spencer in the UK.[13]

The bureaucratic aspects to this tradition emerged during both world wars, where welfare and personnel staff were concerned to enforce minimum standards, to enforce rules on attendance, and timekeeping, and to interpret state regulations in the direction of labour and evacuation.

Larger organizations extend lines of communication, and as more people are employed, policies have to be developed which will cope with people, rather than with individuals. As groups of companies have been formed, a coordinating body is necessary to ensure adherence to policies and hence procedures for the interpretation of rules are promulgated. Collective bargaining over a widening range of issues has led to the formalization of agreements and the 'policing' of these agreements to prevent ad hoc changes which undermine management's position. The increase in employment legislation has also tended to make some companies more formal in their relationships, and more cautious about granting unbridled power to line managers.

In many companies, the problem for the Board is how to keep strategic control over where the organization is going. To do this requires a system of control over the strategic resources of the company, especially its people.

The degree to which personnel specialists exercise control over people for whose work line managers are accountable clearly reinforces the separation between the personnel function and the day-to-day business of the company. Similarly, standardization of working conditions, pay, and job descriptions introduces a formality into relationships which makes it difficult for managers to be flexible in meeting changes in demand, customer requirements, or new methods of operating. Arising from this conflict of interest, distinctions emerge between the espoused personnel policies, and the operational personnel policies.[14] Espoused policies are those policies which are published, or acknowledged officially by management. 'Operational' policies reflect the reality of what happens on the shopfloor, where policies are often ignored or adapted to meet the immediate needs of operations for which managers and foremen are rewarded.

The professional tradition
The idea of personnel management as a profession has been fostered by the Institute of Personnel Management (IPM) since 1945. Stimulus for the 'professionalization' of personnel management has also come from inquiries into management problems, such as the Donovan Report (1968), and the reports on local government and on the administration of the health service.[15] The IPM has also acted as an agent for the occupation, proselytizing the professional cause.[16] The basis for the claim to professional status seems to be the use of social science knowledge and specialized techniques. One of the difficulties is that the study of sociology and psychology has not typically been for managerial purposes. The great

thinkers in these fields, such as Weber, Durkheim, Parsons, Simmel, Freud, Jung, Adler, and more recently innovators such as George Kelly and Eric Berne, did not see themselves as partial to any particular cause, except the cause of science itself. They wished to remain as value-free as possible, and to enquire into the human condition in order to extend the knowledge of our own species.

It was partly as a result of criticism of the social sciences that the IPM changed its examination syllabus in the 1970s and along with many practising managers, gave up the struggle to find congruency between the practical techniques of personnel management and the philosophical undertones of social science. With an increasing momentum, successive governments have introduced new legislation about employee relations. As a source of expertise for personnel staff, this is most welcome. The claim to professional status requires the provision of some kind of 'magic' – and employment law provided a new language, a new outside reference group with whom the personnel specialist could associate. Recently, the IPM has sought to specify minimum standards of conduct, for example in recruitment, and redundancy.

There are still a number of problems with the claim, however. The 'client' whom the personnel specialist is serving can be individual workers, chief executives, line managers, groups of workers, or all four. Conflicts of interest and the possibility of personnel work becoming separate from the business may create difficulties for personnel people. The techniques which have been developed can seem to serve ends in themselves. Job evaluation schemes for example are often expensive to introduce and maintain, yet it is difficult to prove how a new scheme will improve business performance.

As the education and training of personnel managers becomes more specialized, they may find it increasingly difficult to contribute to business planning, and to appreciate the requirements of the market place. Few training schemes address the problem of how to undertake the role, or how to integrate personnel aims with the business.

Models of personnel management

Certain common strands have developed from these different traditions. In each tradition, personnel specialists played little part in the planning of human resources on a long-term basis, although the manpower control and professional traditions offer scope for doing so. The separation of personnel from the purpose of the business prevents an integrated human resource plan from being created.

The professional tradition and the manpower control tradition favour extensive policy formulation, and power granted to personnel departments, which may exert executive control over line management. The welfare tradition emphasizes a reactive approach, with a distance placed between personnel and line management, with minimal policy formulation. The industrial relations tradition also grants policy formulation to line management and ensures that policies are developed around existing institutional arrangements. The approach to change is therefore cautious. Where movement is possible, this might be achieved by informal means, with ad hoc actions at a local level, based on tacit understandings and minor variations to rules.

Taking a contingency view of organizations, we can see how different traditions in personnel management have developed within organizations. The 'welfare' tradition lends itself to organizations employing female labour, with little tradition of trade union representation. Similarly, smaller, paternalistic enterprises would find this tradition compatible with the prevailing management style. Essentially, personnel officers from this tradition serve line managers, and may only adopt more purposeful policies by indirect means, either to enhance their power, or to do good by stealth.

Personnel officers in the industrial relations, or manpower control traditions are most likely to be found in larger organizations, where the trade unions are stronger, and where there are more complex structures. Large public sector bureaucracies, and many of the medium to large companies in engineering, manufacturing and printing, would normally derive much from these traditions.

The 'professional' personnel managers may be more at home where there is an attempt to set up and pursue personnel policies, with board level approval, and where there is change and growth in the organization. Many personnel staff draw on the 'professional' tradition, however, to sustain themselves in the middle-level personnel jobs, found in most medium to large organizations, where what is required is the capacity to undertake work of a 'technical' personnel nature (such as manpower planning, job evaluation, recruitment, or training design and instruction). A few draw on this tradition when operating at the strategic level in organizations of all sizes, when pushing through organization development schemes, for example.[17]

The roles of personnel specialists are therefore not just dependent on their level in the hierarchy. The expectations held about personnel staff are conditioned by the traditions from which personnel management has emerged.

If we think of a continuum of approaches to personnel management, we can distinguish the different 'models' of personnel work adopted by organizations, by reference to a range of internal factors. These are: the decision-making approach of the top management team, the planning time adopted for personnel activities, the degree of discretion exercised by the personnel specialist and the extent to which such specialists are involved in creating the organization's culture, with the concomitant styles of management expected by top managers and employees. This continuum approach to personnel management is represented in Figure 1.

Little discretion	Some discretion, within	High discretion
Short-term planning	limits	Long-term planning
horizon	Medium-term planning	horizon
Gives service to junior	horizon	Acts as consultant to
line managers	Gives service plus advice	senior managers
Gives administrative	to middle management	Conceptualizes
support	Provides knowledge of	Inventive, creative
Follows routines	systems and IR practice	problem solver
Looks for leadership from	Follows systems and	Changes routines/
fellow managers	modifies to some	systems as necessary
	extent	Copes rapidly with
	Gives leadership within	change and leads/
	existing structures	participates with top
		management team

Figure 1

If we think of personnel management contributing to the building of the business, we may use an analogy drawn from the building and civil engineering profession to characterize these three approaches.

Thus, our architect is the long-term designer and planner, creative, flexible and mindful of the need for change. The architect is able to conceptualize and to establish his expertise with client line managers. The expert on the existing contract, ensuring that every sub-clause is fulfilled, is the contracts manager. His knowledge of the system and his pragmatism, his reputation for getting things done quickly, effectively, and for maintaining the existing relationships, grants him a senior job where top management want the here and now well controlled, irrespective of the future. Where all that is expected of personnel is the day-to-day operation kept on schedule, a 'clerk of works' approach is all that is required, where representation of the client line managers' interests is total and unquestioning. Providing as he/she does, technical expertise at the level of routine but important tasks, such as recruitment and forming contracts of employment, the 'clerk of works' approach to personnel management ensures the fulfilment of the immediate tasks – there is no interest in looking at the long-term needs of the business. In our analogy therefore we have

'clerk of works' – 'contracts manager' – 'architect'

Throughout the book we will be using these terms as a kind of shorthand, to represent the models. In the remainder of this chapter and in Chapter 3 we wish to set out the implications of each of these models of personnel management artd to look at their relevance as the twentieth century draws to a close.

When looking at how accurately we are able to assess the contribution of personnel policies to business objectives, the model adopted in the organization seems crucial. We believe that the major stumbling block to achievement of recognition, and success in personnel, is the reluctance of senior managers to be explicit about their expectations of personnel managers. This makes the accurate assessment of personnel management impossible. Without the capacity to demonstrate a relationship between their work and the goals of the business, personnel managers have difficulty in gaining the necessary credibility.

We have suggested that there are in reality three clear models of personnel management which have currency in the United Kingdom today. These three styles have a commanding analytical position but they are not finite – we do not suggest that one of these three will apply wholesale to every organization, every form of organization ownership, at discrete moments in an organization's life. Rather, these are templates which most commonly reflect the operating styles of personnel management functions and personnel practitioners. Each model will have its own variants. The models expressed here are pure forms in the Weberian sense – that is they are broad categories which encompass a specific range of actions (intended behaviours) and which imply roles for personnel managers and their subordinate staff in each case. These roles can be defined as a number of consistent expectations about how they will act in the situations to which they are usually exposed.

These models are found in most industries, in the public and private sectors. What is proposed is that although there are many distinctions between personnel departments, there are tendencies in the decision-making of organizations, and the way specialized personnel staff are expected to act, that produce an approach to personnel management which our models describe. We do not suggest that there is a 'good' and a 'bad' model, but we do argue that the models can be unsuitable, or irrelevant, in a particular organization, at a specific moment in time.

The 'clerk of works' model
All authority for action is vested in line managers. Personnel policies are formed or created after the actions which demonstrate the need. The policies are not pre-set nor are they seen as an integral part of business policy.

Managers in these situations take complete control of the people reporting to them, exercising almost total power over their future, their rewards and the work they do. The only check is the extent to which senior managers take action over the heads of their subordinate managers.

The chief executive may take on the main personnel policy direction and with his immediate reference group develop any tactics towards employee relations. The tactics will be framed to achieve short-term goals, and will not be set out in a policy document.

Personnel systems are created in an ad hoc way. The main systems will require the recording of information after the decision is taken, collecting information together and providing whatever standard letters or statements, are thought necessary. These will probably be the minimum required by law and will be subject at each stage to scrutiny by senior line managers.

The main systems in use will be those generated for financial information; for example payroll, head count and performance against budget will be reported on at senior management meetings.

The Personnel Department will administer basic routines undertaking record keeping, first-interviewing some applicants for employment, preparing letters and documents on instructions. In some companies the welfare role – sick visiting, interviewing employees with problems designated by their supervisors as 'welfare' problems, etc – may be well developed.

If a 'personnel officer' is employed he or she will report to a senior manager (for example, the works manager or chief accountant) and will probably have no specialist qualifications. The most likely career path is from another junior post in the company (e.g. secretary, wages supervisor, etc.), or the person may have been appointed to this role from outside – as a newcomer to personnel work, be it ex-services or from a similar background.

The 'contracts manager' model
In this organization we would expect to find well established personnel policies. These may have been created and sustained by employers' associations and would derive from traditional industrial relations practices. This role would be found typically in the industries heavily penetrated by blue-collar trade unions in the private and public sectors – or in local government, and large bureaucracies, both where the personnel systems are underwritten by industrial relations traditions and practices, or by well established systems.

Line managers perform the main industrial relations activity and have grown up and developed within the system. They therefore see this as the only way to manage. Trade unions have a high density and senior managers connive at maintaining the status quo with local shop stewards and/or district officials. Relationships are very controlled with the accent on procedures for the resolution of discipline problems, grievances and disputes. There are formal bargaining and consultation systems, with an 'espoused' and an 'operational' industrial relations policy. The 'game' of the old hand practitioner is to achieve the latter without disturbing the former.

Personnel staff are specialists with tightly controlled, clearly defined roles. Their activity is mainly in the interpretation of existing procedures, agreements and contracts, although they do make minor modifications to these, adapting to new circumstances (for example, new products, new occupations). A high value is placed on formal trade union/employer relationships and new developments (such as new technology agreements) are debated seriously by senior management with an input from specialized personnel staff.

Personnel officers are usually qualified and their main achievements are in the pragmatic resolution of day-to-day problems. The resolution of immediate difficulties in relationships takes precedence over other issues. Time horizons for planning are in the one to five year range. The accent is on making the existing system work better. Trainee personnel staff are given only a limited area in which to be creative and thus a cadre of like-minded personnel staff is developed – they are rewarded for their technical skill in keeping the existing system operational, not for being risk-takers.

The 'architect' model

Managers at senior level take business decisions in the light of the consequences for the management of people. There is often senior representation of specialized personnel management at board level and at directors' meetings there are regular contributions from personnel specialists.

The corporate plan is prepared with people consequences in mind and explicit links are made between the corporate plan and human resource/manpower planning: human resource planning is designed into the corporate plan.

A creative role is expected from the specialist personnel staff. Policy changes are initiated by the personnel department, which is expected to scan the environment and then to foresee how likely changes will affect the company (for example, in hours of work, externally, or the need to create more job satisfaction, a pressure from internal sources). As with the 'contracts manager' model, personnel specialists are expected to foresee connections between proposed actions and likely reactions of employees. The personnel role is used fully when changes are planned and personnel managers act as partners with senior line managers to produce orderly changes (for example, in divestment, expansion or when new products are to be made).

The industrial relations strategy is explicit and seeks to create new relationships or to build on existing relationships. There may be collective bargaining or no trade unions representing the workforce, but there will be strong values held by the management team about managing people.

The personnel manager regards himself as a business manager first and a 'professional' personnel manager second. This specialist, the architect looks for business opportunities to exploit through the people employed in the enterprise.

There is, however, a 'professional' application to personnel work and technical competence is expected. In particular, the 'architect' may offer the use of diagnostic skills and problem solving, conflict reducing techniques, for example team building, coaching, counselling, negotiation skills and third-party interventions.

The personnel department in this situation would typically evaluate policy proposals in business terms, taking a medium to long-term perspective (five years plus). Thus no proposal that did not have a pay-off in greater productivity, improved quality of work or reduced costs would be thought worth pursuing. However, costs could be interpreted broadly, in terms of social costs and on a long time perspective.

A number of distinguishing features are present in the models we have described. These are represented in the following summary tables.

First model of personnel function: 'clerk of works'

Policies	Not pre set nor integral to the 'business'. Stem from chief executive.
Policy/planning horizon	Short-term, immediate. Emphasis on budgets, not on corporate plans.
Authority	Vested in line managers.
Control	Line managers wholly control subordinates. Only modifying influence: higher line managers.
Systems	Ad hoc, related to legal requirements. Payroll based.
Personnel activities	Largely routine, person not business centred. Routine administration, welfare, selection of junior staff.
Personnel reporting	To senior line manager, e.g. works manager, company secretary.
Personnel career path	From another post likely on promotion, e.g. wages clerk, senior secretary, training instructor.
Political position	Not an issue normally. May be used by other office politicians however. Personnel officers in this model will usually avoid conflict. At a time of upheaval in the company, their strategy will be: 'duck below the parapet. Keep your head down.'

Second model of personnel function: 'contracts manager'

Policies	Well established, often implicit, heavy IR emphasis, employer association derived.
Policy/planning horizon	Short-term, possibly one to two years.
Authority	Vested in senior line managers, personnel authority as 'agent'.
Control	High trade union density, senior manager and local shop steward/full time official connivance. Lowest-common denominator relationship. Balance actually in favour of informal understandings.
Systems	Will be sophisticated systems usually to help with negotiations, and 'manuals' of rules etc. Personnel systems probably work efficiently. Espoused policies.
Personnel activities	Support to senior line management; degree of independence on highly local issues; high interpretative role; involved in formal relationships but not power-broking.
Personnel reporting	Likely to senior line manager, e.g. works manager, but possibly to chief executive. Will anyway be used as 'leg man' and will service authority accordingly. Policeman role.
Personnel career path	'Junior' personnel staff still drawn from other functions, more senior staff start to become professional specialists; selection on the basis of day-to-day crisis management skills; resolution of immediate problems; narrow base of operation.
Political position	Derives from dependent 'agent' position and technical knowledge. Power from operating the system; limited creative role. May become heavily involved in 'plots' and 'counter-plots', because of reliance on informal understandings, and ambiguity of status and authority.

Third model of personnel function: 'the architect'

Policies	Explicit policies giving effect to the corporate plan, concept of human resource planning.
Policy/planning horizon	View of tactical and strategic horizons. Interpretation of corporate and human resource plans.
Authority	Personnel presence at highest levels, people as 'business' resources.
Control	Personnel and line managers move towards extensive integration, rational decision taking obviates need for traditional idea of control.
Systems	Tend to be sophisticated, procedurized. Concepts of human resource planning, manpower information system extensive. Not focused on relationships.
Personnel activities	Personnel manager sees himself as a business manager; looks for business opportunities which make maximum use of people skills available. Technically competent and skilled in diagnostic techniques.
Personnel reporting	To the chief executive.
Personnel career path	Both 'full-time' career professionals and a sufficiently high status function to attract line managers permanently or for a spell.
Political position	Derives from contribution to the business and quality of that contribution. Able to coexist with equality at highest levels. Will have to engage colleagues in the political arena. Power broking will be open. Conflict may also openly break out.

The perceptions of the personnel role by those who assess it are crucial. Difficulties for personnel managers can emerge therefore when either their perception of the role is not shared by senior manager colleagues or where they wish to change the role from 'clerk of works' towards 'contract manager' and 'architect'. In Chapter 3 we will illustrate the working of these models in ways which the experienced reader should find credible.

Notes

1 We are following here the 'action frame of reference' in our discussion of organizations. A definition of the action frame of reference is found in D. Silverman, *The Theory of Organizations* (London: Heinemann, 1970), Chapter 6.

2 B. Wilson, 'The role of the personnel function in a changing environment', in M. Thacker, J. Bristow and K. Carby (eds), *Personnel in change*, (London: IPM, 1978).

3 S. Tyson, 'Personnel Management in its organizational Context', in K. Thurley and S. Wood (eds), *Industrial Relations and Management Strategy* (Cambridge: Cambridge University Press, 1983).

4 R. Harrison, 'Understanding your organization's character', *Harvard Business Review* (May 1972).

5 H.A. Clegg, *The System of Industrial Relations in Great Britain* (Oxford: Clarendon, 1972).

6 J. Child, 'Quaker employers and industrial relations', *Sociological Review* (November 1974).

7 S.M. Herman, *The People Specialists* (The Hague: Alfred Knopf, 1968).

8 A. Fox, *Beyond Contract: Work, Power and Trust Relations* (London: Faber, 1974).

9 M. Niven, *Personnel Management 1913–1963* (London: IPM, 1967).

10 E. Wigham, *The Power to Manage* (London: Macmillan, 1973).

11 Royal Commission on Trade Unions and Employers Associations 1965–1968, *Donovan Report*, Cmnd 3623 (London: HMSO, 1968).

12 E. Jacobs, S. Orwell, P. Paterson and F. Weltz, *The Approach to Industrial Change in Britain and Germany* (London: Anglo-German Foundation, 1978), p. XVIII.

13 W.J. Reader, *Imperial Chemical Industries* (London: Oxford University Press, 1975).
   D.C. Coleman, *Courtaulds, An Economic and Social History* (Oxford: Clarendon Press, 1969).
   G. Rees, *St. Michael – A History of Marks and Spencer* (London: 1969).

14 C.J. Brewster, C.G. Gill and S. Richbell, 'Developing an analytical approach to industrial relations policy', *Personnel Review*, vol. 10, no. 2(1981).

15 Royal Commission on Local Government in England, Cmnd 4040 (London: HMSO, 1968).
   Department of Health and Social Security, *The Future Structure of the National Health Service* (HMSO, 1970).

16 T. Watson, 'The professionalization process: a critical note', *Sociological Review* (August 1976), p. 601.

17 M. Thakur (ed.) *Personnel In Charge* (London: IPM, 1978).

3
The Contribution of Personnel Management to the Organization

What do personnel managers do?

The work of personnel managers is within organizations. In the sense that they are expected by colleagues, superiors and the workforce to represent the organization's norms and values, their work is organizational work. In this chapter, we seek to set out some of the consequences of this fact of life, for the three models of personnel management we have just outlined. We are especially concerned to discuss here the question of how personnel management contributes to the survival of the organization and to what extent personnel roles are boundary roles, interacting with the social and economic environment on behalf of the organization. We will, therefore, discuss the personnel policies which stem from these roles and the strategic significance of personnel management.

We should first be quite clear about what it is personnel specialists actually do. There is no shortage of prescription about personnel work. Each year brings some new magnum opus to an already impressive array of British and American texts which describe the content and techniques of personnel management.[1] The majority of such books rely on an approach originally developed by Moxon, where the activities of personnel management are listed, usually without reference to the needs of the business, or the culture of the organization.[2] The problem facing authors when writing textbooks is that unless the model of the personnel department has been defined (that is, unless the role of the department, the expectations held about personnel work, and the involvement of personnel specialists in decision-making have been set out), they are left with generalizations, and are unable to discuss *how* the personnel policy objective can be achieved.

In the early days of personnel departments, activities were sometimes grouped under the conventional headings, following the subdivisions in the literature. Moxon's categories of: employment, wages, joint consultation, health and safety, welfare, and training are more usually now classified as

Employment	Manpower planning, manpower control and utilization.
Recruitment and selection	Preparation of job descriptions and person specifications, advertising, search consultancies, testing, interviewing and placement, promotion.
Rewards	Job evaluation, salary/wage structures, administration and rules on variance of pay, benefits, conditions of service.
Employee or industrial relations	Collective bargaining, joint consultation, employee communications, employee involvement, administration of procedural and substantive agreements.
Training	Apprentice and other training schemes, management development, induction training, on-the-job programmes, programmed learning, administration of training.
Appraisal	Employee appraisal schemes, systems for identification of training needs, and for identifying potential for giving feedback and monitoring performance.
Health, safety and welfare	Statutory and other safety schemes, safety committees, employee health schemes, and welfare facilities.

Some commentators include topics such as organization design and job design (including job enlargement, job enrichment schemes) under the rubric of the personnel department. In other instances, these topics are seen as part of organization development, which is perceived to have a wider applicability to the concerns of line managers, whatever their functional specialism.[3] The conclusion we may draw at this point is that there is ample discussion about what personnel specialists *ought* to do, and little about what they *actually* do.

The most detailed recent study of personnel activities was undertaken by Guest and Horwood.[4] This consisted of a comparison of two organizations from private and non market sectors in which they checked 85 separate tasks, under 12 activity classifications:

1 Direction and policy determination
2 Planning and research
3 Industrial relations and collective bargaining
4 Pay and benefit determination
5 Payment administration
6 Organization design and/or development
7 Manpower planning and/or control
8 Personnel information and records
9 Employee development and training
10 Recruitment and selection
11 Employee communications
12 Health, safety and welfare

The most common tasks performed in both organizations were:

1 Managing subordinate personnel staff
2 Providing advice to line managers on law
3 Processing job applications
4 Interviewing candidates
5 Taking part in selection decisions
6 Making offers of employment

Perhaps of greater significance than the similarities, were the differences between the organizations. In the manufacturing company, personnel staff were engaged in the full range of advisory, executive and administrative activities. In the health service organization, in addition to the usual staffing activities, the personnel specialists were more involved in policy-making and planning. Neither of the organizations studied conformed to the conventional wisdom about reporting hierarchy in personnel, of personnel director, corporate personnel specialist, personnel manager, personnel assistant. Job titles and position descriptions were too varied for this to be the case. However, the report concludes that many of the personnel managers studied were true generalists covering large numbers of tasks in many different areas of activity. In both organizations personnel managers were primarily attending to industrial relations tasks, whereas their subordinates were more concerned with recruitment and selection.

Who creates personnel policy?

During the 1970s, the idea of appointing someone onto the Board of Directors, to take a general responsibility for personnel and industrial relations, gained favour among larger companies. We must make the distinction between large, multi-establishment organizations, and smaller or single establishment organizations. To add to the difficulties of generalization, there is evidence that some establishments that are part of larger conglomerates operate independently in personnel matters.[5] Certainly there was evidence during the 1960s that many personnel managers did not play a major part in determining industrial relations policy.

We also find Winkler, in his research, suggesting that senior directors intentionally distance themselves from the workforce.[6] He regarded the appointment of personnel directors as either a facile response to worker demands, or a method of bringing personnel staff under cost control. As there were no personnel directors in his study, his comments on the strategies of 'isolation' and 'ignorance' may be more pertinent. The logic of such role definitions, he points out 'permits compromises at a low level on an apparently pragmatic basis so that positions are not yielded in principle'.

If neither personnel managers nor senior directors are active in creating industrial relations policies, the question remains, who is? One answer is that senior line managers, especially in production units are probably the most directly interested members of management.[7] However, we must again be wary of generalization, since personnel departments may be active in backroom research, and briefing, involved in creating the industrial relations climate, while line management undertake the face-to-face negotiations. Industrial relations strategies may not be explicitly formulated and may intentionally be brought into being through an evolving, emergent process, where the part played by individuals is difficult to see.

Writing more recently, after an extensive survey of senior management's role in industrial relations, in manufacturing companies, Marsh confirms that there is no uniform pattern, but in over 70% of multi-establishment companies and divisions 'it is the most senior line manager rather than the personnel specialist who is regarded as having general responsibility for employee relations'.[8] Larger companies do seem to be more likely to use personnel specialists at senior levels, and few major multi-establishment companies are now without a main board director with head office responsibility for employee relations.

One of the most notable findings in Marsh's study was that the main personnel topic for discussion at Main Board meetings in the companies he studied, whatever the size, was company pay awards, followed by industrial disputes and pay systems. By contrast, manpower planning, communications and labour markets were not frequently discussed. Personnel policies as a whole are not often discussed at board level. This seems to indicate the directors' preference to look outwards, away from the organization, towards the market and the business environment. This seems to confirm the findings of successive writers on British industrial relations, that directors only get interested in their employees when there are major costs imminent. Non-board personnel specialists may be influential on the implementation of strategies for change, however.

A recent study confirmed this role for central personnel departments which increasingly are concerned to act in a broad advisory role, while divisions are given more autonomy in the creation of local policies, with executive authority over people matters passed back to senior line management, as part of the move to make local divisions accountable for results.[9] At the 1984 IPM Conference, the Personnel Director of Allied Breweries explained how essential it was to decentralize personnel with personnel directors appointed to local breweries to encourage them to make their own decisions.[10]

What conclusion should we draw from these studies of personnel activities? One of the main conclusions is that there are a number of different ways in which personnel work is conducted, and that we cannot generalize sensibly about 'personnel management' outside the organizational context. There are different models of personnel management. Industrial relations has historically been the responsibility of senior line management. Where senior personnel staff or directors are appointed, this becomes their chief concern. There is an increasing trend to appoint personnel directors, especially in large multi-establishment companies. The responsibility for policy is shifting in two directions: upwards to the board for industrial relations policy and pay, which is still dealt with pragmatically, and reactively, and downwards to individual companies and divisions, where there is no pressure for consistency, and no requirement to establish an overall organization culture. The management of the change process now involves personnel managers in creating transition strategies, and building the people up in the business, as part of a team, working together towards business objectives.

In the three models of personnel management we have outlined, we have emphasized that there is no one model which is ideal for every organization. However, there is still the question of how the models operate within organizations, and at this point we must consider whether more than one model may coexist, at different levels within the same organization. One could envisage the personnel director acting in the 'architect mode', the plant personnel manager as the 'contracts manager', and the junior personnel officer or personnel assistant as the 'clerk of works'. By the 'organization', we mean the unit (which could be a company, a division of a large group, or a branch of a company) which has the responsibility for devising and controlling its own personnel policies.

Different sub-units of a company may adopt different models of personnel management if they have sufficient autonomy in personnel matters. The coexistence of different models in the same organization can be a source of conflict and confusion. There is no direct relationship between the occupational level of the personnel staff and their vision of the personnel function. A personnel assistant, for example, may have been recruited with an 'architect' view of personnel management, whereas the personnel director could have been promoted from long experience of running industrial relations to be personnel director, with a 'contracts manager' perception of the function. Different models may also be found in the same organization where an attempt is being made to introduce a new model. We thus have a time dimension to take into account. In all these situations, we can anticipate conflict, and difficulties in relationships, emerging from the powerful influence of differing expectations. The approaches to personnel management represented by our three models have a presence in the personnel policies pursued by the organization. Personnel policies interrelate so closely that should the models vary at different levels in the hierarchy there will be a perceived dissonance between the objectives and the modus operandi of the various members of the personnel department.[11]

It might seem that where the personnel staff take responsibilities for groups of people there is the opportunity for different models to coexist, for example, where all monthly paid staff have one set of conditions of service, while hourly rated employees have another. However, we must remember here that our models describe approaches to personnel work, rather than just its immediate content. A 'clerk of works' approach may be adopted towards hourly rated or senior staff, just as the way a junior personnel officer approaches the task of negotiation, or of recruitment, could be similar to the approach adopted by the personnel director. The approach to personnel management can be applied at any level in the hierarchy or to any group of people. A personnel assistant in the architect model acts in a strategic way when assisting in the recruitment of a marketing manager, for example, or when interpreting the salary or wages policy which has strategic objectives. By contrast, a personnel director in the 'clerk of works' model might be defined by his colleagues in such a way that all he is left to do is administer the pension fund, and undertake routine procedures.

This leaves us with the question of how do these central tendencies arise in organizations? The organization context seems to be of supreme importance for the emergence of a model seen as appropriate by the client groupings whose interests the personnel specialists serve. Conflicts between models, therefore, do exist, but one would expect some attempts at resolving these conflicts in favour of one model or another. Organizational expectations have to be altered if change is to be accomplished. Later in this chapter we describe in detail the roles available for the personnel department which are functional for the organization. These roles include opportunities for the personnel manager to act as a change agent.

Personnel policies and personnel strategies

Thurley and Wood distinguish between the usefulness of strategic industrial relations thinking, and the analysis of the factors which influence industrial relations strategies.[12] There seem to be a range of contextual factors within organizations which influence employee relations strategy – including the strength and type of trade union organization, the type of technology and the effect of product and of labour markets on the organization.[13] In addition, cultural and social factors are decisive. Operating a personnel department in the Mid East, for example, is rather different from running a department in London. One source of conflict within multinationals is the application of inappropriate strategies, devised in a headquarters and applied in a different country.[14] We can see how, using the broader term 'employee relations strategy', both the 'architect' and 'contracts manager' models of personnel management are associated with the creation of strategies, which have different purposes.

'Organization development' is a term which describes an overall philosophy, embracing a process which has similarities to our 'architect' model of personnel management. One definition of OD, relating it to personnel management, declares: 'Basically it focuses on assisting individuals, groups and organizations to learn how to develop, rather than relying on formal training for individuals, and seeking expert advice for organization improvement'.[15]

The OD work of the 1960s and 1970s tended to draw on the socio-technical systems approach, and used the opportunities provided by technological change to institute changes to the social system of the organization, through re-designing the organization structure, re-designing jobs and applying ergonomic techniques. Often there was an element of employee participation in these schemes.

Emerging new technologies are now causing a new interest in OD. Robotics, computer-aided design systems and new information technology pose problems for the management of people. There is now the prospect of people being supervised by robots. There is fear, anxiety, and stress stemming from the pace of change itself, and by the loss of work identities. There are also trade union battles to be fought over new agreements.

Although there is too little survey evidence to be conclusive, the authors are aware of a substantial number of cases where managements have made broad attempts to overcome industrial relations 'problems', with long-term objectives in view. These could be described as 'transition strategies', as the problems are frequently defined as managing a major change in the company. As Thurley and Wood have pointed out, strategic thinking is only credible 'if the industrial relations strategy is justifiable by its relationship to a clear and acceptable business strategy'.[16]

We can illustrate how the recession has forced many organizations into formulating a coherent business and employee relations strategy by the case of British Shipbuilders.[17] Faced with the worst recession experienced by the shipbuilding industry, high material and labour costs, together with better organized overseas competition, British Shipbuilders has had to review its technology, the organization of work, and the methods of management. The strategic response to these problems has been to institute a 'common-core' technology, including administration, labour cost controls, financial controls and computer-aided design and computer-aided manufacturing systems. The new approach, which involves designing for production, more standard components, modular assembly and the creation of work stations (with work station drawings and materials packaged for each station), requires a constant team of people, and imposes considerable changes on technical personnel who now have to work as part of a team. Changes in attitudes are fundamental to the success of the programme, and considerable effort has been put into communicating these changes. A new 'philosophy of work' – called 'accuracy control' – has been instituted which has elements of employee involvement, and which requires each individual worker to 'sign for' his work. New training policies, harmonization of pay between monthly and hourly-rated employees, and more employee involvement, especially to explain the 'how' and 'why' of change, are the main personnel policy outcomes of this strategy. Other examples could be found in other parts of industry and commerce. In the case of British Leyland, a more explicit industrial relations strategy has been deployed, with the intention of creating a set of relationships compatible with management objectives.[18] We would see both British Shipbuilders and British Leyland as cases where the recession has forced the company to move from a 'contracts manager' towards an 'architect' model.

We have already commented on the way that formalization in personnel policies arose as a consequence of larger, more complex organization structures, where central personnel departments were established to ensure that a network of policies stemming from the centre was carried through, as exemplified by those following the merger which created ICI in 1926.[19] This is a good illustration of the way that structure follows the business strategy. Personnel policies emerge from the strategy, therefore and help to establish the formal structure of relationships in the organization, and a 'culture' or 'climate' in which such a set of relationships may flourish.

Lawrence and Lorsch have noted that as organizations become more differentiated to cope with the requirements of the market place, so there is a greater need for integration of the company's activities if the organization is to survive as a unit.[20] Personnel policies in employment, industrial relations, staff development, and rewards are often designed to prevent the centrifugal force of profit centres from pulling the company apart. This crucial aspect of the personnel role is brought into focus when companies sub-divide into divisional units. Personnel policies frequently perform latent functions for organizations, as for example when management development policies are used to create a common management 'culture', by lateral transfers and the inculcation of a common management ideology through training.[21] Personnel policies thus are significant determinants of 'culture'.

Williamson and Ouchi argue that organization strategy and structure are explicable by reference to the governance of contractual relations, and to the transaction costs involved in those relationships.[22] The distinction that they make between 'hard' and 'soft' contracting has a bearing on the three personnel management models. In 'hard contracting' the formalization of relationships forces a reliance on procedures and a legalistic interpretation of the employment contract. The parties to the contract are more autonomous, and jobs are very task-specific. 'Soft contracting', on the other hand, relies more on tacit understandings, and a reciprocal sense of obligation. Work is less clearly defined, and there is a reliance on personnel policies to support the relationships. In an extreme form, the distinction could be drawn between hiring someone to paint one's house (hard contracting), and employing an odd-job man whose duties include house painting, gardening, etc., on a regular basis, and who is virtually a personal servant of his employer (soft contracting). It is contended that organizations which operate soft contracting require a highly organized internal labour market with defined promotion systems, training policies, job evaluated payment systems, as part of an elaborate 'informal governance apparatus'.[23]

The concept of hard contracting is therefore not unlike our 'clerk of works' model, or our 'contracts manager' model. Similarly, soft contracting could be related to either a 'contracts manager' model, or to the 'architect' model, depending on the strategic purpose of the 'soft contract'. Where there is an intention to create soft contracts for a business purpose, and the personnel manager is able to act as a supremo of the internal labour market, we would see the model in the 'architect' mode. The promulgation of corporate values is a central role for personnel management in establishing the 'clan' on which the policies depend for their acceptance.[24] Corporate values are pervasive, and are central to the creation of organization cultures.[25] Such values when expressed through organization cultures prescribe appropriate relationships and specify the legitimacy of actions.[26] The organization's reward and punishment systems are the means by which these central values are seen. The promotion, appraisal and development policies of an organization are influential in this regard. In addition there are more subtle influences, where policies indirectly affect the culture, including the way the tasks are done and the priorities are set.

A recent study of personnel policies in non-union companies in the USA demonstrates the centrality of values for employee relations strategies.[27] The study discovered that top management motivation was crucial among the internal company factors that keep a company non-union. This was either 'philosophy laden' with well thought out beliefs about the treatment of employees, often articulated in writing, or 'doctrinaire', which contained union avoidance programmes, deriving from a fear of union pressures. A part of both these approaches was emphasis on personnel management, consistent with 'soft contracting'. The formalization of the role was most noticeable where the founder's influence had diminished. After the founder had left, the 'audit and control' role of the personnel department was critical for the success of the employee relations strategy. This entailed the personnel department reporting to the chief executive, or to a staff vice-president, with deep involvement in policy creation. The 'audit' role necessitated personnel staff educating line management in the running of the broad strategy.

Organizational roles

From our brief description of how personnel policies are generated, we can see how the department becomes 'functional' for the organization. We would argue that there are four major roles that personnel managers should play within organizations. The roles are

1   To represent the organization's central value system;
2   To maintain the boundaries of the organization;
3   To provide stability and continuity; and
4   To adapt the organization to change.

There is a similarity here with the functional prerequisites adumbrated by Talcott Parsons – who claimed that for an organization to survive and perform its function, it must adapt to its environment, maintain the role systems of the organization, integrate the parts of the organization, and that the parts should identify with its goals.[28]

1   To represent the organization's central value system
The lack of power exercised by personnel managers can be overcome, according to Karen Legge, in one of three ways.[29] Personnel managers may become convergent innovators, seeking to introduce changes congruent with senior managers' value systems, or divergent innovators who would establish the relevance of different values and try to convert managers to them, or a 'problem-solving' approach could be adopted which is akin to the personnel manager acting as an internal consultant. Legge's typology shows the political nature of organization decision-making and demonstrates how the main chance of influencing the process rests on how the personnel manager approaches the value position of his colleagues.

Most of the decisions in which the personnel manager could influence the strategy of his or her company are 'non-programmed decisions', that is, they are about new events, new policies or reactions to the behaviour of people.[30] These decisions seem to depend on 'judgement' or 'insight' of an undefined sort, and thus are value-laden in the extreme.

A number of writers have commented on the political nature of organization decision-making, but we would also stress its lack of a prior rationality.[31] As a part of the decision-making team, the personnel manager is in a position both to influence the values of his colleagues, and to be the principal organ representing these values to the people who work for the organization. He may also be expected to represent them in a public relations sense to the world outside, alongside his colleagues in marketing and sales. For example, the Personnel Director of IBM is director of corporate affairs with a strong public relations responsibility. As an example of the negative case the personnel manager of a large pharmaceutical company was recently dismissed by the general manager, as it was claimed he failed to represent the company in a favourable way to a newly appointed manager during an induction interview!

One way of exerting influence over the top management team is for the personnel director or his equivalent to become the close 'confidant' of the managing director. Personnel directors are often regarded as being sufficiently neutral, compared with their marketing and production colleagues, to be able to offer unbiased advice on the way the company is organized, and to act as a friend to the chief executive. This is useful for the isolated chief executive who may want to discuss his director colleagues with someone who can provide informed comment on their personality and management style.

We have seen that the choices that are made of a strategic nature greatly affect personnel policies in employee relations. This is also true of the recruitment, training and management development areas. The commitment to the organization's goals, the degree to which people are involved in the business, and the extent to which rewards are shared often derive from these choices.

The organization's central value system is the collective expression of the ideology of the senior management. It can be seen as

a A reflexive process answering the question, what does the company represent itself to be to the world at large? Corporate images are sometimes expressed through slogans which become catch-phrases for staff and customers alike, and express organizational values. The John Lewis Partnership – 'Never knowingly undersold' – gives an impression of honesty and fair dealing. The New York Times – 'All the news fit to print' – stands for propriety and openness, and IBM's 'IBM means service' is a further reinforcement of the significance of customer relationships.

b A reciprocal process, as the implicit statement of what the company stands for in order to evoke a sympathetic response from those who work for the company. For example, the Marks and Spencer recruitment brochure describes the fundamental principles of the business and goes on to say, 'A strong theme running through these principles is communication – the need for close understanding and cooperation between company and our suppliers, the management teams and staff in our stores, between stores and head office, and the communities in which we trade. Reacting in a dynamic way to help promote healthy communities makes sound business sense.' It would seem essential that those who are engaged to work towards broad corporate objectives should share similar priorities and should interpret the world in a similar way. In practice, it may only be the management and a proportion of non-supervisory grades who do share similar values.

2 To maintain the boundaries of the organization
There are a number of ways in which personnel managers fulfil this role:

a Through their activities in designing organizations, and by helping to frame the rules governing the internal structure of the organization they set up the boundaries. These can be quite

intricate since many companies nowadays are part of complex
structures, with subsidiary boards, sometimes operating
multinationally. Rules governing the internal structure determine
levels of authority. These rules are framed both in a purposive way,
when changes are planned, and as the consequence of other actions
such as job evaluation programmes and job enlargement and job
redesign schemes.

b One of the most important aspects of personnel work involves the
creation, change and termination of contracts of employment. The
rules of work are also part of the output of personnel departments.
These rules help to provide the sense of there being an
'organization' in existence. The rules are set out so that they derive
from logically developed reasoning, and thereby a rational belief is
created in their absolute value.[32] In any organization, managers are
concerned to maintain their power so the legitimation of their
authority through legal/rational means, maintains a sense of order
and structure, and delineates the boundaries between work and non
work.

As concepts of work are changing so the management of the
boundaries of the organization requires greater ingenuity. For
example, modern information systems open up possibilities for
working at home, the use of self-employed contractors is now more
common, and there are changing concepts of career with which
personnel staff must cope.

c As we have seen in our discussion on values, the personnel function
helps to sustain an organization's sense of identity. In particular we
would mention here its social rather than its legal identity. Personnel managers act on behalf of the company towards employees,
and in the reward, the training, promotion and recruitment policies,
for example, an organization's culture is sustained. The culture is
also generated by the feelings of employees, as an attractive, or a
fearful environment, as an exciting or a dull place to work. What we
are stressing here is the process of sustaining the organization in a
particular form, which is congruent with the preferred style of
management and of structure. This process can be observed in the
control exercised over communication channels or when a central
personnel department exercise power over a local unit's personnel
department to ensure obedience to a central management edict.

In their study of six different factories, in the engineering,
clothing and process industries, Edwards and Scullion report the
workers views of management.[33] The majority were either neutral,
with phrases such as

'They don't bother you' or
'We see little of them'

or were adverse, as expressed by these quotations:

'Distant from the shopfloor'
'Strict and unfriendly'
'Inconsistent'
'Don't know the job'

As the researchers note, in all cases, it was management's control systems which were the key to understanding the attitude of the workers. They remind us that both workers and managements are pursuing strategies. Workers' strategies to limit output, or to retain control over the pace of work, might be countered by changes in the bonus system, absenteeism by new timekeeping rules for example.[34] There is thus a 'frontier of control' being moved back and forth between the two opposing groups. From their research, it would seem that where managements are able to produce an individualized rather than a collective response from workers, then management are able to exercise a greater degree of domination over the work-force. This corresponds to the findings in the study of personnel policies in non-union companies in the US quoted earlier.

A central role for personnel management here is to help secure a high level of effort for a given wage. On a broader front, personnel policies which help to create trust (such as openness about rewards, rational promotion procedures and the like) are also influential. One significant finding from the Edwards and Scullion study was the revelation that workers' judgements about their managers' competence influences their motivation. Managers who are unable to make accurate predictions about the product market or who are indecisive are as demotivating to workers as managers who are authoritarian and insensitive.

3   To provide stability and continuity

a   This role follows on directly from the one described above. The voluntary tradition in British industrial relations, where the legal framework is largely concerned with individual rights and with stipulating the immunities trade unions have from prosecution, dictates that personnel managers provide stability and coherence for industrial relations at the organizational level. In some industries, employers' associations still help in this role but company level bargaining is now most common. Uniquely among managers, personnel executives give considerable weight to the history of the organization and particularly to the history of relationships. Many managers are, of course, great repositories of company history, norms and traditions, but for the personnel manager, the history of the organization and the mores of its inhabitants are of crucial concern to his work.

b   Industrial relations policies require a continuity of purpose on the part of the company and a continuity of relationships between the executives responsible for industrial relations and trade union officials and lay representatives. Such stability helps to ensure a sense of fairness, and helps to avoid the creation of unfortunate precedents. It also reinforces the notions of rationality we outlined above.

c   The coherence between personnel policies must also be maintained as a part of their role. This inhibits rapid changes of policy and helps to make for a more cautious approach to the management or relationships.

d   Personnel policies on succession, and on training are also aimed at keeping a stable set of relationships. Succession planning and development policies ensure the continuity of certain key management activities.

The British Government's handling of trade union membership at GCHQ illustrates the problems managers face if they suddenly change policy, so that all the taken-for-granted assumptions about managements' intentions towards its employees are called into question.[35] In this case, two years after the trade union at GCHQ had engaged in industrial action, the Government decided to ban employees there from trade union membership, with an offer to 'buy out' their memberships with cash payments. Since the Whitley system was established in the early 1920s successive governments had sought stability in their relationships with their employees and continuity in their agreements, and hence had encouraged trade union membership. The sudden reversal of policy is a cause of great bitterness, which is still continuing through legal actions at the time of writing. What has upset the relationship so much is the abandonment of the normal role of personnel management, which seeks to maintain stability and continuity, so that social life may proceed.

4   To adapt the organization to change

Personnel managers, as much as any managers, are acutely conscious of the effects of change on their companies. The increasing pace of change is itself a major problem. Since the end of the Second World War, economic pressures, such as those caused by full employment, have determined reward policies and have made managers more aware of the significance of industrial relations decisions. Of equal significance have been changes to the society at large in which organizations operate. New technology, changing standards of education, new attitudes towards the balance between work and leisure, more foreign travel, more consumer goods, increased house ownership, better communications and a host of other transformations to our everyday existence, have taken place in recent years.

a   The role here of the personnel department is to ensure that the modernization of the organization's approach towards its employees takes place in ways that are appropriate. The change agent role is performed through personnel policies in such crucial areas as employee relations, reward structures, selection, promotion and management development.

The move towards single status, new incentive payment systems such as value added schemes, employee involvement and communication techniques for example, can give powerful leverage to the process of change. A major management development programme encompassing all the managers in an organization is potentially the most compelling way of stimulating change. New ways of behaving, new techniques to apply and a different attitude or outlook on management should derive from a programme aimed at revitalizing the management team.

For this role to be successfully applied, the personnel function requires representation at the strategic level of decision-making and integration between corporate and human resource planning. The more successful companies have always tried to plan for change in this way. For example, the human resources planning process adopted at General Electric in the USA entails an environmental analysis and resource analysis.[36] These are compared with the business strategies which identify any major discontinuities. Following the analysis, plans are made to exploit any opportunities and to overcome limitations on future operational plans. Although such planning is never perfect, it should provide a coherent approach, allow the necessary coordination and it does permit the preparation of contingency plans to prevent failures in operation.

b   It is not possible for managers to act towards employees without acknowledging influences beyond the factory gates. When we define our lives in a social sense, we define also our obligations towards others.[37] Since work is a social process, the fact of working gives us these obligations. There is, therefore, a felt need by managers for channels of communication with society.

The need for a societal strategy for the firm has led to a project undertaken by the European Foundation for Management Development, where the argument has been advanced that the stakeholders in society – managers, government, unions, shareholders, large institutions, mass media and various others, are growing in importance and power.[38] What one might call 'the lobby' is extremely active, at company policy level: employers' associations, ecology groups and consumer associations – political parties even – are often seen to be actively concerned in policy-making. Phillipe de Woot has suggested that firms need a 'societal strategy' to avoid 'the development of a socio-political gap which is too large and which will result in a risk of economic decline'.[39]

To try and match the value systems of the various stakeholders is a task for the whole senior management of the enterprise but because of the role of personnel in monitoring the core value system, it is the personnel function which can play an important part in matching the values of the stakeholders with the values of the firm, or of coping with the dissonance.

For the organization to survive it must reflect changes in society as a whole. We can illustrate how personnel staff act as a medium for exchange by reference to changes in employment law. The law is an index of social change and recent developments have provided personnel staff with major tasks in converting old practices into new. For example, we would cite the Health and Safety at Work Act 1974, the changes in discipline procedures following the unfair dismissal legislation, the Equal Pay Act, and the sex discrimination legislation as instances of new standards demanded by the public to which staff managers must respond.

Similarly, the legal changes are often only a part of a wider social change; for example, in the status of women. Issues such as increased concern over sexual harassment at work and equal opportunities in training and promotion reflect the need for personnel staff to act as a medium for bringing change into the organization.

In their policies for training, and for managing change itself, personnel staff try to adjust not only the formal approach to these new requirements but also to help individuals to adjust to new ways of living and working. By this process, personnel managers help to change society and thus we may speak of an exchange between the organization and the wider community.

We have now set out the four roles personnel managers can perform to ensure the survival of their organizations. When we compare the extent to which each of the three models can fulfil the four roles, a number of distinctions can be seen and it is clear that it is only in the 'architect' model that all four are adequately covered (see Figure 2).

	Represent central value system	Maintain boundaries	Provide stability, continuity	Adapt the organization to change
'Clerk of works'			_____	
'Contracts manager'	_____			
'Architect'	_____			

Figure 2

In the 'clerk of works' model of personnel management, we would find the main organizational roles in the routine work on maintaining the organization's boundaries, for example in forming contracts of employment and on the detailed interpretation of policies which characterizes the role of providing stability and continuity. Although personnel managers within this model would empathize with the decisions of senior management, they are only required to represent these decisions in a routine way. In spite of a narrow remit, there are opportunities to aid the survival of the organization even if these are restricted to performing these roles at a mechanical level.

'Contracts manager' personnel departments will try to keep abreast of the values of top management and may influence them in favour of the industrial relations which seem essential for survival. One would anticipate most senior managers to be in favour of stability and these top management values may be used by the personnel manager to reinforce his own power and to make adjustments to policy in response to new problems. As we have outlined in the 'contracts manager' model, personnel managers concentrate on the provision of stability and continuity for the organization.

Personnel managers following the 'architect' model will major on their opportunities within the 'change' role, to influence the other three roles. They will ensure that they are closely associated with management decision-making and will be a party to the formation of managerial values.

Changing from one model of personnel management to another means changing expectations. The four organizational roles of personnel management which help the organization to survive can be performed in a way which changes expectations, either by bringing into consideration factors from the wider society or by emphasizing the strategic elements of the role. Only the 'contracts manager' and 'architect' models seem to possess the credibility for such an involvement with the crucial tasks of the organization.

Summary

In this chapter we have sought to show how the three models of personnel management relate to personnel policies. We have described how no one model is suitable for all organizations, and for all time. The question of which model is appropriate for any particular organization can be answered only in terms of the roles we have defined. The expectations of senior management are the determining factor, and these expectations of how the personnel job should be done will dictate the personnel policies.

We have also indicated in this chapter how different models may produce conflict among managers. When considering the four roles we have identified as functional for the organization we must also accept that there are potential conflicts of objectives between them. Managing change and providing stability and continuity are, at first sight, mutually exclusive. However, the four roles described, with all the contradictions and conflicts, do occur within the everyday activities of personnel.

One of the authors of this volume recalls how he was required to manage the redundancies of a central stores unit employing 250 people, on the condition that the stores continued to operate at full efficiency up to the last minute when all its work was transferred to sub-units throughout the UK. In one sense, continuity of the stores work had to be ensured while the major change took place. Managing such contradictory objectives seems to be quite normal in personnel management. The contradictions are frequently between means and ends.

The inherent conflicts within all the personnel models adds to the difficulties of evaluation. The 'welfare ethic' of caring for employees, according to their needs, and helping them to develop according to their talents must live side by side with the work ethic, which places a moral value on hard work, thrift and monetary success. Personnel policies frequently lag behind business objectives. It is not unusual for example to find organizations, having adopted policies which are designed to retain people, and to reduce labour turnover, having to encourage voluntary redundancy and natural wastage, in order to meet a change in the company's fortunes.

From these conflicts over the model of personnel management, the roles of the personnel department, and the mixed and changing objectives which must be accommodated by personnel policies, personnel staff are often perceived to be occupying an ambiguous and uncertain position. This is an issue we must address when formulating methods of evaluating personnel work.

Notes

1 Since there are so many books on the market which cover roughly the same ground – there are at least 12 British and American texts readily available – we must assume this is a popular subject. Perhaps the most well known in the UK are G. Thomason, *A Textbook of Personnel Management* (London: IPM, 1976) and subsequent editions and D. Torrington and J. Chapman, *Personnel Management* (London: Prentice Hall, 1983).

2 G.R. Moxon, *Functions of a Personnel Department* (London: IPM, 1951).

3 The Work Research Unit of the Department of Employment, for example, is concerned with all the traditional areas of OD, and on the whole addresses the line manager rather than the personnel specialist in its publications.

4 D. Guest and R. Horwood, *The role and effectiveness of Personnel Managers: A Preliminary Report* (Department of Industrial Relations, London School of Economics, 1980).

5 J. Hamill, 'Labour relations decision-making within multinational corporations', *Industrial Relations Journal*, vol. 15, no. 2 (1984).

6 J. Winkler, 'The ghost at the bargaining table: directors and industrial relations', *British Journal of Industrial Relations*, vol. 22, no. 2 (1974), pp. 191–212.

7 Royal Commission on Trade Unions and Employers' Associations 1965–1968, *Donovan Report*, (London: HMSO, Cmnd 3623, 1968).

8 A. Marsh, *Employee Relations Policy and Decision-Making* (Aldershot: Gower, 1982).

9 See Harrogate Report, *Personnel Management* (December 1984), p. 18.

10 ibid., p. 19.

11 We should perhaps here recall the significance of differences of opinion about the relevance of the model adopted by the National Coal Board in the view of its Industrial Relations Director, Ned Smith. See S. Tyson, 'Is this the very model of a modern personnel manager?', *Personnel Management* (May 1985).

12 K. Thurley and S. Wood (eds), *Industrial Relations Strategy* (Cambridge: Cambridge University Press, 1983), p. 203.

13 D.R. Deaton and P.B. Beaumont, 'The determining of bargaining structure: some large scale survey evidence for Britain', *British Journal of Industrial Relations*, vol. 18 (July 1980).

14 The problems of cross-cultural policy-making and some examples are discussed in P. Hesseling, *Effective organization research for development* (Oxford: Pergamon Press, 1982) and in M.J.F. Poole, 'Personnel management in third world countries', *Personnel Review*, vol. 11, no. 4 (1982).

15 J. Bristow *et al*, 'An introduction to organization development', in M. Thakur *et al*, (eds) *Personnel in Change* (London: IPM, 1978), p. 25.

16 Thurley and Wood, *Industrial Relations Strategy*, p. 223.

17 *Performance Improvement and Productivity – A New Shipbuilding Strategy*, British Shipbuilders internal document (July 1983).

18 P. Willman and G. Winch, *Innovation and Management Control. Labour relations at BL Cars* (Cambridge: Cambridge University Press, 1985).

19 W.J. Reader, *Imperial Chemical Industries: A History* (London: Oxford University Press, 1975).

20 P.R. Lawrence and J. Lorsch, *Organization and Environment* (Cambridge, Mass. Harvard University Press 1967).

21 S. Tyson, 'Management development as a part of organization development', *Management Monitor*, vol. 3, no. 2 (November 1984).

22 D.E. Williamson and W.G. Ouchi, 'The markets and hierarchies programme of research: origins, implications and prospects' in A. Francis, J. Turk and P, Willman (eds), *Power, Efficiency and Institutions*, (London: Heinemann, 1983).

23 ibid., p. 27.

24 A. Fox, *Beyond Contract: Work, Power and Trust Relations* (London: Faber, 1974).

25 G.W. England, 'Personal value systems, so what?', unpublished paper, University of Minnesota (1973).

26 R. Harrison, 'Understanding your organization's character', *Harvard Business Review* (May 1972).

27 F.K. Foulkes, *Personnel Policies in large non-union companies* (New Jersey: Prentice Hall, 1980).

28 T. Parsons, *The Social System* (Glencoe, Ill.: Free Press, 1951).

29 K. Legge, *Power, Innovation and Problem Solving in Personnel Management* (London: McGraw Hill, 1978).

30 H.A. Simon in *The Shape of Automation for Men and Management* (London: Harper and Row, 1965), pp. 57–79.

31 A. Pettigrew, *The politics of organizational decision-making*, (London: Tavistock, 1973).

32 M. Weber, *The Theory of Social and Economic Organizations* (New York: The Free Press, 1964), p. 60.

33 P.K. Edwards and H. Scullion, *The Social organization of Industrial Conflict* (Oxford: Basil Blackwell, 1982).

34 ibid., p. 167 *passim*.

35 R. Long, 'Comment', *Personnel Management* (April 1984).
'GCHQ' stands for Government Communication Headquarters.

36 J. Baughman, 'Human resource planning at General Electric', *International Management Development Quarterly Review* (Summer 1982).

37 E. Durkheim, *The Rules of sociological Method* (New York: The Free Press, 1964).

38 'The European Societal Strategy Project' as reported at 1982 EFMD Annual Conference.

39 P. deWoot, 'Towards a societal strategy for the firm: a discussion' *International Management Development* Quarterly Review (Summer 1982), pp. 24–29.

4
The Personnel Management Occupation

The writer Jan Morris evokes powerful imagery in relating the final days of her passing from manhood to womanhood. Climbing high into the mountains of North Wales, where the

> chimera, half male, half female . . . [could bathe alone] . . . and all alone in that high world, stand for a moment like a figure of mythology, monstrous or divine, like nobody else those mountains have ever seen. . . .[1]

Androgyny may not be the identity crisis of personnel managers but the chimera as a simile has its appeal. The profusion of identities is in part self-inflicted. Personnel managers inadequately articulate an identity, a coherent statement of their contribution to an organization's attainment of its objectives, perhaps because their contribution is so diffuse, and difficult to evaluate in financial terms. They are faced with doubts about their effectiveness and with uncertainty about the criteria used to judge success.

Departments which provide an indirect service must expect to come under pressure to justify themselves at a time of recession, when costs are constantly scrutinized. The position of the personnel department is particularly vulnerable since its work does not possess the machismo image of a sales department competing for orders, or of a production department organizing the output. In some cases, the recession has pushed personnel activity into the background, granting it low priority, as the following quotation from a personnel director testifies:

> Ten years ago, my department seemed to make all the running; virtually nothing happened without our involvement. But now we have to fight just to know what's going on.[2]

The problem is that not only have many of the traditional concerns of personnel been put on the back burner, but the recession has given some line managers a chance to change the very character of the personnel policies themselves. Many managers, seeing high unemployment levels, have been tempted back towards 'hard contracting'. Divestment of business, sub-contracting and less concern with policies designed for labour retention have gone hand in hand with the Government's privatization of state-owned industries, and the return to reliance on 'market forces'. The labour market has become more fragmented in recent years with the growth of part-time employment, sub-contracting, and short-term employment contracts.[3]

'Soft contracting' implies a feminine image, a compromising stance predicated on techniques which create harmonious working arrangements. In soft contracting, the personnel department typically seeks to manage an internal labour market. As we explained in Chapter 3, soft contracting may be chosen as a strategy which seeks to control relationships, and to prevent trade unions from obtaining members in a company. The soft contracting approach may accord with the values of senior managers. The resistance to soft contracting and the reactionary forces against it, however, have an opening provided by the defensive stance of organized labour, and the high levels of unemployment. Many line managers would see no necessity now for the panoply of personnel policies supporting soft contracting. When faced with industrial conflict, the reaction of such managers is to 'tough it out', as was seen in the British miners' strike of 1984. We are in an era of 'give-back' bargaining, the concessions now are sought from the workers, not from management. Any uncertainty or lack of confidence displayed by personnel specialists can be interpreted as confirmation that they contribute little to the business compared with the costs of their policies.

A number of authors have commented upon the ambiguity inherent in the personnel job.[4] Our purpose in this chapter is to examine the debate on ambiguity, and to discuss how personnel specialists may demonstrate their functional roles. 'Demonstrating' a role implies that personnel people will need the skills to carry senior management with them to a better use of the people employed by their organizations.

Most of the criticisms of personnel are based on the assumption that really, the emperor has no clothes. The 'professional' image is seen either as a smokescreen or as a strategy for survival. Our counter to the charges against personnel management will be to describe how the framework of knowledge, skills and techniques necessary for personnel specialists are dependent on the model of personnel adopted by the organization's members, and to show we can evaluate its contribution. We will begin by examining the professionalization of personnel management, to see how the professional tradition has influenced the question of the ambiguity of the personnel role.

The personnel manager as a professional

We discussed the 'professional' tradition in personnel management in Chapter 2, where we saw how this tradition emerged after 1945. The issue of 'professionalization' is important because we may discover more about the occupational identity personnel managers possess by discovering the values they espouse, the way they regard their work and the image they wish to create.

The extensive literature on the study of 'professions' is dogged by problems of how to define the word 'profession'.[5] The two most common approaches are firstly a list of traits, or characteristics, the possession of which denotes a professional status, or secondly definitions which relate the concept to the study of elites, class structure, and the ways in which groups obtain a high status in society. Studies of 'professionalization' as a process of socialization, describe changing views of self as the 'traits' are acquired.

Research into personnel management as a profession has formed a basis for a number of occupational studies. In the USA, Ritzer and Trice submitted that the way personnel managers were treated resulted in different sorts of commitment, either to the organization or to the 'occupation'.[6] According to Watson's opinion, the adoption of the professional image is a strategic response by personnel specialists to their felt lack of authority.[7] His judgement that personnel management is an emerging profession, with an ideology based on the application of social sciences knowledge, which demonstrates its contribution to organizational goals, legitimating the specialists position, is akin to Legge's 'conformist innovator'.[8] There are similarities between Legge's views and our own. Her thesis: that there are different approaches to the idea of professionalism, according to the organizational context, is useful since at least it draws us back to a more appropriate level of analysis.

We do not believe that the notion of being a 'professional' is as important to personnel managers as the studies quoted so far would lead us to believe, however. Research by Tyson indicated that the organizational context of personnel management is a crucial determinant of the occupational ideology.[9] The organization is the only real source of status and rewards. Personnel managers, of all managers, must be seen to be 'organization men'. There is no real evidence of a strategy as a whole. Proof of such a strategy would have to show that across all the different companies and industries personnel specialists were acting in concert to fulfil some sort of chosen destiny to which they all subscribed. The only indication of a group of personnel specialists acting together is found in the Institute of Personnel Management, the activities of which could not be described in this Machiavellian way.

We do not question that there is a broad occupational identity, although there are several such occupations covered by the umbrella term 'personnel'. Personnel management is seen as a career option by students seeking employment; advertisements appear with broadly similar duties under the title personnel manager, and research for the classification of occupations showed that the title has common usage.[10] In his research into the views of 100 personnel managers, Watson mentions how the title 'personnel manager' had achieved general recognition.[11] We feel confident that there is an occupational identity, therefore, but that does not justify the assumption of an occupational strategy. Furthermore, it is our view that there are significant variations in personnel management, deriving from the different models of personnel management adopted by organizations.

This still leaves the question of how important is the IPM in creating a status grouping out of the various occupations which come under the rubric of 'personnel'. There is no doubt that the IPM seeks to sustain the formally acknowledged status of personnel management as a profession. Its activities as a qualifying association demonstrate how a small group of people have set out and sustained an organization in order to perpetuate the claim to be professional.

In addition to any substantive benefits, the officials of the IPM are likely to obtain improvements in the image of the IPM by, for example, engaging in national debates with the CBI, the Government and the Manpower Services Commission, and by acting as a pressure group. The claim for professional status has been made by leading members of the IPM in their regular journals, and through other media, such as newspapers, conferences, and training courses. By setting examinations for membership, the Institute's supporters are able to have some regulatory function, and to give new members a rite of passage, and a common source of status in the Institute. The branch network provides members with contacts and a local presence of the Institute, and with opportunities for information sharing. At first sight, therefore, the IPM might seem to be very influential.

There is evidence, however, that the influence of the IPM is not so extensive as its role as a qualifying association implies. Firstly, the majority of the people engaged in personnel work are not members of the Institute. The total membership of the Institute is 23,332 (at June 1984), of whom only about 8000 are corporate members, the remainder being students or affiliates of various kinds.[12] If we estimate the ratio of personnel staff to employees as 1:500, IPM membership must account for only around a half of all those performing some kind of personnel function, that is as a minimum, recruiting, rewarding people, and terminating contracts of employment. Indeed, the position may be worse than that. A recent survey into industrial relations in the UK stated:

> There is no one who spends a major part of their time on personnel or
> industrial relations matters in more than half the 135,000 workplaces which
> employ more than 25 people. Around one-half of the managers who do spend
> a major part of their time on personnel work are not personnel specialists;
> only one-half of the personnel specialists have any formal qualifications for
> the work.[13]

Even where personnel specialists do become members, this does not mean that they are active in the IPM. In a survey commissioned by the Institute, 32% of members said they never attended branch meetings, and there were relatively few regular attenders.[14] Although the IPM does act as a pressure group, no major change in Government policy can be traced to the Institute's intervention. The IPM warned against the provisions of the 1980 Employment Act to no avail, for example.[15]

Our remarks so far have indicated that the IPM has not exactly overachieved as a qualifying association. Nevertheless, the work of the Institute in training and developing personnel specialists has been outstanding. Its publishing activities, and its courses and conferences, have been influential in bringing a much greater awareness of the occupation within management, and in passing on personnel techniques to specialists and to line managers alike. One of the most important benefits to come from the IPM's examination system is the stimulation it has given to personnel training courses at colleges throughout the UK.

The mere organization of the occupation is not itself a criterion for being accorded the title 'professional', according to Millerson.[16] An area of competence, the service ethic, and recognition by both the person himself and by others that he belongs to a profession are essential requirements. To Wilensky, 'The service ethic is the pivot around which the moral claim to professional status revolves.'[17] The institutionalization of the professional status is a means by which the service ethic may be preserved, and the client's interest protected.

The statements by the IPM on the problematic area of the service ethic have revealed considerable confusion.[18] In recent years the personnel manager seems to be encouraged to make the line manager his client, whilst trying simultaneously to represent wider social standards, and to possess a sense of service to employees. This results in confusion and difficulties for the personnel executive.

The connection between the two broad ways of viewing professionalism is the service ethic. It is through the idea of service to others that the values of those who claim to be professional are made a public property. We would argue therefore that the claim to professional status has confused the image. Many personnel managers now have to defend untenable positions due to their separation from the business.

To summarize, what we have described so far is the Anglo-Saxon predilection for self-policing gentlemen's clubs, as a way of controlling ethical standards for professional groups. What was once an organization started by women welfare workers in 1913 is now a male-dominated Institute.[19] The IPM has developed examination schemes, and has had a powerful, and beneficial influence on the training and development of personnel specialists, but it has not been able to restrict entry. In spite of its efforts at image-building, the countervailing power of organization ideologies have frustrated the creation of a separate occupational ideology. The salient difficulty experienced by those personnel specialists who claim a professional status alongside medical practitioners or lawyers, is the absence of an agreed client.

We do not believe that personnel specialists need to claim a societal status separate from their manager colleagues. Since personnel work is conducted within organizations, and in accord with the model appropriate to the expectations of management, the key to success resides within the organization's socio-political structure. This is the structure of relationships and influence groups through which power is sought and exercised.

Power and authority

From the exposition on professionalism we may conclude that the authority of personnel specialists is attributable to their organization position. Senior managers are typically imprecise about how much power to accord to personnel departments, and during sensitive times, such as when there is an industrial dispute, the base line has an awkward habit of shifting. In looking at this question of authority, we must distinguish between power and authority.

Power may be defined as the degree of control over the environment and over the behaviour of others which is possessed by individuals or by groups of people.[20] Leaving aside Adlerian notions of an individual's complexes of superiority or of inferiority, we are more concerned with the power exercised on an interpersonal scale.

French and Raven designated six bases of social power: reward, coercive, legitimate, referent, expert and information sources of power.[21] Personnel specialists potentially have access to all six sources, but in practical terms, their capacity to reward (by formal or informal means), their expert knowledge (for example in such matters as employment law) and their control over information are the most likely sources. Their power is not an absolute, but is a variable dependent on the support granted by colleagues, and by the extent to which the personnel managers control the key axes in the organization: such as recruitment, information sources and communication channels. The amount of power is also a function of the importance of the issue to the organization. Consequently, the closeness of the personnel department's stance to corporate values, the greater the power of its members. The formal position of the personnel department in the organization structure also determines access to these power sources. In this context one sees cases where a senior industrial relations role in head office is created, while decision-making in personnel administration is devolved to units or departments.[22]

Power is made legitimate to the recipients by an acknowledgement that it is being exercised on behalf of a recognized authority.[23] Authority can be legitimized by tradition, by the legal or rational basis for its existence, by possession of expert knowledge, by some moral belief, or by the charisma of the individual who seeks to exercise it.[24] The model of personnel adopted by the organization is crucial for an understanding of the disparities in authority.

Model	Authority source
Clerk of works	Traditional or moral
Contracts manager	Legal/rational and/or charismatic personality
Architect	Expert knowledge and/or moral

These typologies offer a differentiated view of personnel management and authority. In our 'clerk of works' case, personnel managers will operate within prescribed limits, established by tradition. This is not to imply that the 'contracts manager' and 'architect' operate with impunity outside the norms, rather it is a comment on the 'clerk of works' particular tendency to operate wholly within accepted formal and informal guidelines. A primary consequence is an exceedingly narrow span of decision-making power for the latter. In this role, he or she will offer a routine service, based on what is accepted unquestioningly as administrative support. His or her counsel and advice will not be sought but, rather like the traffic warden, there will be an uncompromising statement of the possible and the prohibited. This could originate from the belief system in the organization, which has moral force, and is thus unchallenged.

In this environment, the personnel manager's patronage will not be solicited by one party or other to a dispute since it is largely an inconsequential asset. All the more ironic, therefore, that if the personnel manager wishes to establish an authority beyond the confines of procedure, he or she will seek to do so by some form of patronage or influence based on the narrow band of discretion which frequently lies on either side of a rule. There is not a large amount of latitude but there might be enough to help a line manager secure his objective – for example to speed up the release of recruitment authorization, or give practical support over a grievance where to the line manager's embarrassment, the complainant might well have good reason to feel aggrieved – and in turn this earns the personnel manager the fleeting gratitude of the line manager.

The 'contracts manager' case will find personnel managers approaching the question of authority with confidence and clarity. In this instance, it is wholly a matter of involving the authority of the office. The quality of the advice, the evidence that the judgements were 'right' over the long term are not substantive issues. In the bureaucracy, the personnel department will have duties to perform and these will have varying degrees of importance to every other function securing their own objectives.

It is in this situation that one finds the personnel function deriving its authority in part from the support given to it by the chief executive, either formally, or a tacitly recognized support, known throughout the organization. Authority here is made legitimate by reference to the rules of work, which this model of personnel creates and maintains.

In the 'contracts manager' case, there is no hesitation. The chief executive will 'use' personnel although the inhabitants of the department may hypocritically lament their being so used. Procedures and rules will be convenient for this exploitation of power. There will be no slavish adherence to them, and there are marginal limits either side. For the majority, the rules and regulations will be seen to suffice, they will deal with the day to day, and they will not be so formalized that a sudden, but expedient action causes a major disruption to the organization.

A different approach in respect of authority will come from the 'architect' model. Here in all likelihood the head of function will be a member of the highest authority-giving circle whatever the formal structure. Power will derive from expert sources: from demonstrable success, from the quality of advice, and action. Innovative goals will have been set for this function. Successful achievement of these goals will both reinforce and enhance the personnel authority. The value of the opinion and the proven quality of decisions taken will be the basis of influence rather than trade-offs and short-term, expedient solutions. Interpersonal dealings among the authority-granting circle will establish a personal position and status which, if performed recognizably well, will provide influencing opportunities. A professed and bona fide interest in the 'business' will increase the legitimation. An organization will often appoint a senior line manager to head up the personnel function on the very premise that this grants legitimacy among the person's peers, technical competence in personnel management being seen as more easily learned later. In contrasting the various approaches to authority sources, an affinity with the business is the primary source of influence and authority for the 'architect'.

This is a useful juncture to restate our original premise. The 'architect', or 'contracts manager', or 'clerk of works' approach might be ideally suited to the organization's expectations of a personnel function. There may be no dissension over what is being provided. The organization and its personnel department may feel entirely comfortable with each other.

One of the principal difficulties faced by all personnel managers is the lateral source of their power. Because they tend to act on behalf of others there is a problem in establishing credibility. There are a number of possible responses.

The 'clerk of works' will no doubt utilize the role of winged messenger to avoid criticism, and to pass on any disapprobation to the boss. Go-betweens often see much of the action from a vantage point not open to the participants, and the clerk of works may therefore become a repository of detailed information. For the contracts manager, access to first-hand employee relations knowledge affords the opportunity to control information which has a strategic value. Information of this kind may be helpful in making predictions about future policies, and the reaction of work people to future plans, and is therefore a powerful resource. There is also the prospect of coercion. For example, in recent research one instance was discovered where the appraisal system was operated by the personnel manager, so that he was able to influence promotion decisions, adversely or otherwise depending on the managers' support of the personnel systems. The architect will use skills as a consultant both to influence line manager 'clients', and to help analyse the situation. With the architect, the problem is to avoid using power acquired by access to strategic decision-making, in such a way that the client – line manager relationships are affected. The degree of trust found in the organization will encourage appropriate relationships, but inevitably the influencing skills of the personnel specialist need to be used to cope with the company's juntas and cliques.

We have already commented on the diffuseness of industrial relations responsibilities. This is not just a British problem. In his splendidly entitled article: 'Big hat, no cattle', Skinner points out that in the USA there are 'critical problems in the corporate management of personnel work, such as the place of human resource management in corporate decision-making', as well as a lack of human resource management know-how at the top levels, which are unresolved.[25]

Credibility with top management

Assessments made of personnel management come from a variety of assessors. We have so far discussed the views of personnel practitioners themselves and we have also commented on the societal position of personnel by looking at the professionalization of the occupation. Most of the assessors of personnel management are within the same employment network. To elucidate these assessments further the authors contacted a dozen well-known companies and sought the assessments of senior managers.

The most encouraging response came from the Chairman of ICI, one of the world's most successful companies, who stated that

The Personnel Department and a proactive leading personnel policy have been the key to the success of our organization over a great many years. We believe that it is only by having the most up to date policies, constantly reviewing them, and introducing new specific aims for our personnel policies that our Company remains a major international operation.

His personnel department is assessed for positive and challenging reasons:

it being their responsibility to operate the development, training and recruitment policies which should produce an adequately prepared personnel resource to achieve the business objectives we have set.[26]

This view was sharply echoed by a former chief executive of a nationalized industry in comparing the purposes and activities of the personnel departments in the 10 companies of which he is now non-executive chairman.

Others have made similar statements about the centrality of personnel

activities to their business. In a recently published series of articles, one
chief executive reminded us that

> In a service industry the most important ingredient in the product is
> people. . .not surprisingly almost every discussion we have in the Company
> starts or finishes with personnel matters.[27]

Another, speaking of the celebrated Japanese experience haunting as it
does his industry – motor vehicles – attributed its success to the 'result of
sound personnel initiatives'.[28]

The viability, if not the prosperity, of the organization turns on the contribution of personnel co-equally to other functions. This was the view
expressed by the recently retired Chairman of Reed International. Among
his 10 firms, personnel was not expected to be, nor perform as being, some
form of appendage, mandated to deal only with 'people issues'. All function
heads were expected to assess the value of their contribution across all
business issues. The evaluation indices were subjective and internal, but
they were more or less consistently applied without too much favour across
all functions. The finance function was seen as having some type of special
relationship – based on its legal responsibilities and control over legally
accountable assets – but if anything the expectations of it were more
taxing and in conversation certainly emerged as more tangible than
personnel.[29]

The ideas which have been expressed are not universal. A chief executive
of a £1 billion company is equally forthright in his view that

> in the past one of the reasons why personnel has often failed to take its place
> at the company's top table has been that its contribution was seen to be impor-
> tant but peripheral to the primary issues of survival and growth.[30]

The effort and quality of the contribution exhibited by personnel practitioners, which has earned them a high place in some organizations, has not
yet permeated to all organizations.

Recent research into 28 case studies of organizations undergoing
restructuring (20 of which were from the private sector) showed that the
responsibility for initiating organization change in most cases, came from
the chief executive.[31] The personnel director typically played only a
facilitating role, as part of the team of senior managers, and assisted the
change by helping to create strategies for redundancies , redeploying staff
and redundancy counselling. The exception was the organization planning
department of the Ford Motor company which was situated within the personnel department and was responsible for the initiation of restructuring
within manufacturing plants. An example of its achievement was the
reduction from eight layers of managers in the hierarchy to five, with
devolution of decision-making, better communication and more clearly
defined accountabilities.

In our discussions during the interviews with senior managers certain of the people interviewed, while feeling strongly about the 'value' of personnel and always placing it at 'the centre of things', were frequently unable to describe any of the tangible assessment methods they applied. When asked – repeatedly 'how' did they in practical terms come to a conclusion about the value of a function at a particular moment, they became vague. How are personnel 'directors' evaluated in performance terms? In one case, the former chairman of the nationalized steel industry – took soundings among his fellow industrial leaders as to what they were *getting out of* their personnel functions.

A recent study, undertaken on behalf of the British Institute of Management, examined the question of what criteria are used to assess the performance of executive directors, and senior management. For most companies, the performance of the board was synonymous with the performance of the company, and the most common measure was the rate of return on capital employed. The conclusions for senior management were that in addition to measures of profitability there were less tangible considerations, such as how the organizational dynamics worked, the extent of team work and staff development, the confidence, determination and leadership of the managers, and their capacity as communicators.[32]

The expectations of line managers about personnel are influenced by their being both fellow employees and potential clients for personnel advice and for the services necessary to perform their own duties. This dual role can lead to experiences of personnel which do not result in over confidence in the quality of any personnel input which might in turn be being applied to the manager's own affairs! Poor advice on a departmental personnel management issue does not engender confidence that one's own affairs are in competent hands.

A recent American study showed that only 34.8% of line managers thought the various functions performed by personnel aided their productivity objectives, 54.3% believed the personnel function had no effect, while 10.9% thought the personnel function *impeded* their plans.[33]

The tensions are felt within the function as well as in relation to other groups with whom the function relates. Personnel as a function may have its own budget accountability for example. In this case the head of function will be as equally charged as others to keep within financial targets. There will be personnel plans which require financing from the same budget. All this is against a backcloth of a demand for assistance which both can be planned and therefore predictable in budget implications or sudden and inescapable irrespective of the budget consequences.

Management and employees as a whole do not articulate their requirements of their personnel function. There is a multiplicity of expectations and many different levels of contribution are needed. This lack of articulation is both a problem and an opportunity.

Role ambiguity and politics

Role ambiguity seems to be inherent in personnel management. The professional role model evokes the image of a person set apart from manager colleagues, with management, but not of management, and the overtones of the early welfare origins reinforces a vision of the intercessory status, between management and work people. Confusion over who is the client compounds the problem. Large-scale organizations create managerial roles which are remote from the working people. Personnel managers usually do not know personally the employees for whom their policies are intended. Much of the time in personnel work is therefore spent in the difficult task of trying to predict how people will react and in coping with contradictory and ambiguous messages about their behaviour. If we define personnel managers as the specialists in the management of the employment relationship, then the continuous negotiation of that relationship leads to the persistent need to reinterpret meanings. In this way, personnel managers have been described by Tyson as 'specialists in ambiguity'.[34]

Power and authority frequently do not coincide in the same role, and ambiguous roles are often stressful to carry out. Objectives for personnel specialists are less likely to be clear than for other senior managers given their involvement in relationships. Watson has commented on how the non-quantifiable and ambiguous aspects of the work provide both a source of ambiguity and are potentially the most rewarding, because they are so close to the heart of the human condition.[35]

The question must thus be raised of how do personnel people cope with ambiguity, and what would we see as the most productive way of handling this inherent problem. Mitroff and Emshoff have pointed to how 'political' behaviours develop from ambiguous situations.[36] Before proceeding we should clarify what are the boundaries of 'political' behaviour.

The influence processes in which personnel managers necessarily engage when struggling with the ambiguities of their roles can readily be defined as 'political', from our experience of 'covert' and what may be perceived as unauthoritative (i.e. non-legitimated) behaviours which therefore have a negative connotation. It would be naive to suppose that our intentions will be accepted unopposed, and that our interests will always coincide with those of others with whom we interact.

In an attempt to develop a theory of political behaviour in organizations, Kakabadse and Parker define politics as 'the resultant interactions that arise from the consistent (or inconsistent) behaviour that an individual adopts in reaction to actual or latent issues in the situation'.[37] They argue that a repertoire of cognitive competencies are developed which enables people to discriminate successful from unsuccessful behaviour strategies, in different situations, and that these 'enactment strategies' are operated according to whether the perceptions are 'inner directed' or 'outer directed'. Outer directed perceptions in this scheme suggests trading on shared meanings, with the organization, whereas those who are inner directed are less dependent on the organization for their values and therefore live with 'unshared meaning'. From this paradigm, Kakabadse and Parker see four approaches to politics emerging, depending on whether the person follows simple or complex enactment strategies, and on whether he is outer or inner directed.[38]

We can relate the four categories which emerge from their work to our models. Their 'traditionalist' who operates with shared meaning and simple enactment strategies is akin to the 'clerk of works' model; the 'company baron' who shares values and meanings with the organization, and conducts complex enactment strategies is similar to the contracts manager; the 'visionary' who does not accept the organization's meanings and operates complex strategies is similar to the divergent innovator as described by Legge, whereas the 'team coach' who has a simple enactment strategy, but who wishes to move the organization with him to new values, and new meanings is like the 'architect' model.

The main weakness of the analysis in terms of four political types is its concentration on the individual in the political process. By seeking personality characteristics to explain political behaviour, the authors have moved away from a study of the alliances, cliques and opposition groupings which earlier writers have identified as the hallmark of political behaviour. Further, the cognitive approach leads Kakabadse and Parker to conclude that all behaviour in organizations is political.[39] Since this robs the word 'political' of meaning we must conclude that the omission of the covert, group aspects of behaviour from their analysis undermines their explanation. In this further development of the cognitive paradigm, Kakabadse reassures readers that political behaviour is not reprehensible, and that the means justifies the end.[40] He illustrates this point by a case study from his own experience as a consultant, hired to change the attitudes of managers in a personnel department. Having concluded that some managers were very resistant to change he told the personnel director a 'white lie', that these managers, were not bad but needed interpersonal skills training. During their training he secretly kept a copy of personality and other tests which he later sent to the personnel director with a 'hit list', recommending that the managers he found troublesome be transferred out of the department, to which the personnel director agreed.[41] One may be forgiven for discerning in such accounts an attempt to turn duplicity into an art form.

No one can deny the value of the managerial skills required to get ideas accepted: to persuade, present, and to put forward a cogent argument. Personnel managers in particular require such skills because they are so often dealing with the intangible, the ambiguous aspects of management. However, we believe that it is because personnel specialists are dealing with human beings that political skills must be tempered by ethical considerations.

Personnel managers walk a tight rope because they work at the nexus of competing values. Their task in exacting effort from employees brings them into the major questions about the work ethic – the moral value of hard work for someone else in return for wages. The struggle between expediency and goodness, which is a central debate in Western philosophy, is thus at the heart of the ambiguity felt by personnel managers. It is, perhaps, best expressed by Socrates in Gorgias:

> All the other theories put forward in our long conversation have been refuted, and this conclusion alone stands firm, that one should avoid doing wrong with more care than being wronged, and that the supreme object of a man's efforts, in public and in private life, must be the reality rather than the appearance of goodness.[42]

This is not to suggest a moral purpose for personnel work, but it does point to the responsibilities which go with high corporate office – responsibilities which extend to the wider society than the shareholders, customers or one's own boss. Nor is this just a question of corporate image. It is futile for us to bewail the violence, corruption, fraud, cruelty and cheating of our urban Western society if we ourselves are not prepared to behave by a code of high ethical standards. Society is not only 'out there', it is within us, and is structured by our actions, our policies and our intentions.

In a study of student members of the IPM, Tyson presented the students with a hypothetical conflict over a recruitment problem, in which they were asked if it is legitimate for a personnel manager to represent a job as being permanent, although he or she knows it is only temporary, in order to fill a vacancy quickly.[43] For most students, the thought of being openly dishonest was too much, and they felt strongly enough to say that they would resign rather than give in to the senior manager. When pressed, however, a number of strategies were put forward, in an attempt to compromise. This tendency to shift and turn between different criteria when faced with conflict has been noticed in other studies of personnel staff.[44]

A survey by Slater investigated whether redundancy criteria varied by size of firm, and between service and manufacturing industry and whether personnel managers saw any differences between the 'real' and the most 'fair' policies.[45] Although there were significant differences according to size, there was some general agreement that the choice of who to make redundant would most likely be 'bad workers', the over 65s, and those last in. They also agreed that the categories actually chosen in their experience were the most 'fair', a result that Slater explained by the social status of the managers. He argues that they share similar values to other managers, values which are consistently different from those held by individuals at lower levels in the company.

Earlier descriptions of the development of specialist management saw a neutral management élite emerging from the separation of ownership from control. In Berle's view, personnel departments were created as a part of this emerging sense of social responsibility, to help balance the claims of the various stakeholders.[46] However, managerial attitudes towards industrial relations have, in more recent research, been seen as consistent with a 'neo-laissez faire strategy'. In a 1980 survey of 1058 managers drawn from the BIM's membership list, managers typically sought curbs on the existing activities of trade unions, alongside a reduction in levels of government intervention in other areas.[47]

The evidence that being a member of the management team is an important part of the self-image of personnel specialists stems from a number of sources.[48] Entry to personnel work (which seems to be typically not a first choice of career) is often from other managerial posts, and from what is known of personnel managers, they usually come from a middle-class background.[49] In Goldthorpe's terms, personnel managers would seem to have a bureaucratic, instrumental attachment to work.[50]

Personnel managers are facilitators. Their work allows other managerial work to happen, and their professional expertise should therefore be directed at this purpose. All managers could be said to be discharging a latent societal function. The unintended consequences of the personnel role include helping to socialize people into the organization culture, helping to extract the maximum effort from workers at a given cost, and thus they are part of the control apparatus of those who deliver products or services in the economy. But since work itself is a social activity, the way the process is conducted is crucial to the well-being of all in society. The ambiguity of the personnel role can lend itself to political manoeuvring, as we shall see in Chapter 5.

Ambiguity can also be used purposively, not as another political ploy, but as part of the skills used to change meanings. We may all be involved in some manipulation in our relationships, but we can, at least, try only to use that manipulation in a positive way. Personnel managers can avoid a negative, bureaucratic reaction to ambiguity, in which more rules are formulated, and they can also avoid a devious response, which manipulates meanings for their own ends.

> Since meanings are shifting, and being negotiated in the normal course of social interaction, providing the purpose is to ensure the success and happiness of employees, the resolution of conflict, or the development of talents, the manipulation that is involved can be said to be positive.[51]

The reality of professionalism should therefore be in the ethic not in its institutionalization. The professional ethic requires expertise, and a concentration on the skills and knowledge which are needed to achieve work tasks. This sense of the word 'professional' could be applied to all managers.

The social sciences and personnel management

The expertise on which success in personnel management is based origi-
nates from an understanding of individual behaviour and of social action.
Sociology and psychology, which could be described as the explicitly
social sciences, are the academic disciplines which are dedicated to providing this understanding. From our comprehension of action we are able
to predict reactions.

We are not claiming that social scientists possess magical properties.
Rather, we would state that any assumption, expectation or interpretation about one's self or others is by definition sociological, or psychological. The question of how accurate the assumption, expectation or
interpretation is depends on the knowledge and experience of the person
assessing, expecting or interpreting. Sociological or psychological
judgements therefore are not made solely by experts, but are made by all
of us as we proceed about our everyday lives.

We all take a theoretical approach in life. The 'theoretical stance' is our
normal method of understanding. We proceed through common-sense
theories, and tacit understandings which we try out in our everyday existence, and modify according to our experience. A conscious effort is
required to turn our common-sense theories to practical account. Further,
it would seem helpful if we built on the cumulative learning of others, and
tested our empirical discoveries with some degree of scientific vigour. The
process of learning, and testing our ideas about social life is well
expressed by Douglas:

> This means that we definitely must look at the whole idea of taking the theo-
> retical stance toward everyday life as a strategy for progressive 'reductions'
> of everyday life rather than as something that leads us immediately to seek
> *the* fundamental truths about everyday life. We must consciously seek par-
> tial, (objective) truths that will be undone by further reduction or deeper
> analysis of everyday life.[52]

The distillation of experience into meaningful patterns is not exclusively the province of the social scientist, therefore. Experience in line
management can also be used as a basis for generating practical theories,
but above all we need generalizations which can help us to turn our individual experiences into a practical theory.

The personnel manager needs a broad background in the relevant areas
of all the disciplines which can provide a deeper analysis of the employment relationship. Lupton argues for the term behavioural rather than
social science; he suggests that personnel managers should draw on social
psychology, social anthropology and sociology to analyse social situations.[53] Almost any aspect of sociology or psychology could be relevant
depending on the problem. For example, developmental psychologists
have much to contribute to the design and evaluation of training programmes, because they specialize in how people learn and change. Many

of the approaches to problem-solving now adopted have been drawn directly from the social sciences; two examples are non-directive counselling from psychotherapy, and cost-benefit analysis from economics.

It would be impossible for us to detail here all those aspects of the social sciences which have had and continue to have an impact on personnel management. We are robust in our view that the social sciences provide the basis for successful performance in personnel management. Failures in the past are attributable, not to too much social science, but to too little. Ultimately, all economic purposes are human purposes. Personnel managers have the exciting task of translating these economic purposes into human terms, that is into actions which meet appropriate human needs and aspirations. The only tools they possess to do this are their knowledge of business, their acumen, and their understanding of behaviour and of relationships.

The training of personnel managers

The training axiom with which readers may be familiar, is that an understanding of the job is necessary before one attempts to design a training scheme. This knowledge of the job should also include an appreciation of the performance standards required. The IPM's attempts at designing a training scheme which is seen as relevant have suffered from a lack of research in these two vital areas. The evidence for this has come from successive attempts at designing a scheme which avoids criticism. A recent circular from the IPM to course tutors contained the comment:

> The Assistant Director, in talking to students and tutors throughout the UK, often hears the comment from students that the organizational behaviour content of Stage 1 is too 'academic' and not 'relevant' to personnel managers.[54]

The failure seems to lie in the teaching method, which does not show the connections between personnel work and social science, and with a syllabus which has not provided students with a sufficient understanding to make the connections themselves.

Before we condemn the IPM we must recall our previous comments about the lack of clarity in the personnel role. In the case of personnel management we have an occupation where the measurement of performance is extremely difficult, given the imprecision which surrounds personnel work. We believe clarity comes from understanding which model of personnel is to be used.

Given the architect model, we would argue that the approach to personnel training which should be adopted, is for neophyte personnel specialists to be successful managers first, and to be successful specialists in the different areas of the employment relationship second. There is a recognition by the IPM and the colleges which train personnel specialists of the importance of skills training. However, we believe that personnel specialists have no credibility, and no real contribution to make if they are unable to manage people themselves. Managing people is only half the story. Managers have to operate within financial parameters and to achieve output objectives through people. Whatever the model, consultancy skills of varying levels will be required. This leads to more diagnostic skills, and to the development of self awareness, and clarity of purpose.

We would wish to see considerable enhancement of broad management topics within the training scheme and more personnel specialists with line management experience. The general management knowledge should include: marketing and business policy, finance and accounting; operations management, business systems and quantitative methods.

This leaves the question of how can sufficient knowledge of the social sciences be obtained, as well as general management training. We do not see these as alternatives. The work of personnel specialists is sufficiently important, and should be taken seriously by those following the occupation. They ought to be prepared to obtain an in-depth knowledge of the social sciences. What we are recommending therefore, is a degree or diploma level course in the social sciences followed by training in management as an ideal profile for the personnel specialist. We will not dwell here on the personnel techniques which should be acquired. There are many excellent texts in which these are described. What is lacking in many texts is *how* to do the personnel job, rather than what to do. For example, job evaluation schemes are relatively simple to understand but learning which is appropriate, when and how to introduce it is the more difficult, and potentially the more important aspect of the personnel job.

Other writers have stressed the need for personnel to be integrated into the business. Wilson argues that there are new skills required by personnel specialists, if they are to help manage change: skills in the diagnosis of problems, behavioural skills, skills in organization design, role clarification and team building.[55] We have reiterated the business requirements by suggesting general management knowledge, supported by appropriate skills. The 'political' skills should not be used for self-interested purposes, and should be confined to persuasion.

Summary

To reiterate our earlier point, the orientation of personnel specialists is primarily to the organization, which is the source of their occupational identity. Although they have the opportunity to perform roles which are highly functional for the organization, the ambiguous character of their work contributes to the problems of convincing others of its value, and this may result in an excessive use of political strategies by practitioners. What is required of the adept practitioner is how both to sum up the dominant view of what is expected, and to satisfy minority interests.

Ensuring the congruity between what is silently sought by the organization, and delivering it ensures the acceptance of the personnel manager, and a degree of credibility. We would argue that this requires a high level of expertise in the academic disciplines which provide the theoretical basis for personnel management, and the business acumen, combined with broad management training, to integrate personnel activity with the business.

Notes

1 J. Morris, *Conundrums* (Coronet Books, 1972).
2 K. Manning, 'The rise and fall of personnel', *Management Today* (March 1983), p. 74.
3 20% of the workforce is part-time, according to *Social Trends 14* (HMSO, 1983).
   The number of self-employed people is growing by 5% per annum; see *Department of Employment Gazette* (June 1983).
4 T.J. Watson, *The Personnel Managers* (London: Routledge and Kegan Paul, 1977).
   K. Legge and M. Exley, 'Authority, ambiguity and adaptation, the personnel specialists dilemma', *Industrial Relations Journal*, vol. 63, pp. 51–65.
5 For a summary of the study of professions see H.M. Vollmer and D.L. Mills (eds), *Professionalization* (Englewood Cliffs, New Jersey: Prentice Hall, 1966).
6 G. Ritzer and H.M. Trice, *An occupation in conflict. A study of the personnel manager* (Cornell University: 1969).
7 Watson, *The Personnel Managers*.
8 K. Legge, *Power, Innovation and Problem Solving in Personnel Management* (London: McGraw Hill, 1978).
9 S. Tyson, *Specialists in Ambiguity* (unpublished Ph D Thesis: University of London, 1979).
10 *The Classification of Occupations and Directory of Occupational Titles* (London: HMSO, 1972).
11 Watson, *The Personnel Managers*, p. 48.
12 *IPM Annual Report* (1984), p. 10.
13 B. Daniel, 'Who handles personnel issues in British industry?', *Personnel Management* (December 1983), p. 25.
14 K. Baillie, *IPM Membership Survey* (Unpublished report, 1974).
15 See, for example, the *IPM Digest's* numbers 199 (February 1982), 211 (February 1983), and 212 (March 1983).
16 G. Millerson, *The Qualifying Associations* (London: Routledge and Kegan Paul, 1964).
17 H. Wilensky, 'The professionalization of everyone?', *American Journal of Sociology*, vol. 70 (1964), pp. 138–158.
18 Although the IPM issues 'Codes of Practice', they all contain disclaimers, such as the code on redundancy: 'It is recognized that it may not always be possible or practical for employers to follow every recommendation contained in the code.' (February 1984).
19 P. Long, 'Would you put your daughter into personnel management?', *Personnel Management* (April 1984).
20 M. Ryan, 'Theories of Power', in A. Kakabadse and C. Parker (eds), *Power, Politics and Organizations* (Chichester: John Wesley, 1984), p. 21.
21 J.R. French and B. Raven, 'The bases of social power' in L. Cartwright and A. Zander (eds), *Group Dynamics Research and Theory* (London: Tavistock, 1959).
22 I. Boraston, *Personnel Management in a large Metropolitan District Council* (Unpublished Case Study, Sheffield City Polytechnic 1984).
23 M. Weber, *The Theory of Social and Economic Organizations*. Transl. by A.M. Henderson and Talcott Parsons (New York: Free Press, 1947), p. 324.
24 ibid, p. 328.

25 W. Skinner, 'Big hat, no cattle', *Harvard Business Review* (September – October 1981), pp. 106–144.
26 John Harvey-Jones, Chairman, ICI, private correspondence with the authors.
27 R. Forte, 'How I see the personnel function', *Personnel Management* (August 1982), p. 32.
28 G. Turnbull, 'How I see the personnel function', *Personnel Management* (May 1982), p. 38.
29 Sir Alex Jarrett (Chairman of Reed International) in discussion with the authors.
30 Sir Adrian Cadbury, 'How I see the personnel function', *Personnel Management* (April 1982), p. 29.
31 A. Evans and A. Cowling, 'Personnel's part in organization restructuring' *Personnel Management* (January 1985).
32 C. Halley, T. Kennerley and E. Brech, *Management Performance and the Board* (BIM Special Research Project Report, 1983).
33 S.J. Mushkin and F.H. Salter, *Personnel Management and Productivity in City Government* (Lexington Books, 1979); quoted by A. Fowler in *Personnel Management* (May 1983), p. 27.
34 S. Tyson, 'Personnel management in its organizational context', in K. Thurley and S. Wood (eds), *Industrial Relations and Management Strategy* (Cambridge: Cambridge University Press, 1983), pp. 146–156.
35 Watson, *The Personnel Managers*.
36 I.I. Mitroff and J.R. Emshoff, 'On strategic assumption making: a dialectical approach to policy and planning', *Academy of Management Review*, no. 1 (1979), pp. 1–12.
37 Kakabadse and Parker (eds), *Power, Politics and Organizations*, p. 95.
38 ibid, pp. 96, 97.
39 ibid, p. 87.
40 A. Kakabadse, *The Politics of Management* (Aldershot: Gower, 1983), p. 12.
41 ibid, pp. 120–121.
42 Plato, *Gorgias* Trans. by W. Hamilton (Penguin Books, 1960) p. 148.
43 Tyson, *Specialists in Ambiguity*.
44 Ritzer and Trice, *An Occupation in Conflict*.
    Watson, *The Personnel Managers*.
45 R. Slater, 'Who goes first?', *Personnel Management* (December 1969).
46 A.A. Berle, *Power without Property* (London: Sidgwick and Jackson, 1960).
47 M. Poole *et al.*, 'Managerial attitudes and behaviour in industrial relations: evidence from a national survey', *British Journal of Industrial Relations*, no. 3 (November 1982).
48 P.D. Anthony and A. Crichton, *Industrial Relations and the Personnel specialists* (London: Batsford, 1969).
    Watson, *The Personnel Managers*, pp. 88 and 91.
49 A. Crichton, *Personnel Management in Context* (London: Batsford, 1968).
    Watson *The Personnel Managers*, p. 73 and p. 209.
50 J.H. Goldthorpe *et al.*, *The Affluent Worker: Industrial Attitudes and Behaviour* (Cambridge: Cambridge University Press, 1968).
51 S. Tyson, 'Taking advantage of ambiguity', *Personnel Management* (February 1980), p. 45.
52 J.Douglas, *Understanding Everyday Life* (London: Routledge and Kegan Paul, 1973), pp. 34–35.
53 T. Lupton, *Industrial Behaviour and Personnel Management* (London: IPM, 1969).
54 *On course supplement* (unpublished IPM paper, 1984).
55 B. Wilson, 'The role of the personnel function in a changing environment', in J. Bristow *et al. Personnel in Change* (London: IPM, 1978), p. 34.

5
Case Studies of Personnel Management

One of the major blocks preventing personnel managers from demonstrating their contribution is the lack of techniques for assessing the value of personnel work. As we pointed out in Chapter 4 most top executives seem to be vague about how they assess personnel management. In this chapter we wish to demonstrate how assessment is influenced by the model of personnel management the organization adopts and to establish the criteria which can be used in making assessments. We can illustrate the three models by describing case histories drawn from our experience. Following our contingency approach, case studies, rich in contextual factors, provide an apposite method for showing how different elements in the organization's history and 'culture' impinge on the assessment of personnel activities.

The three cases presented below are true. Each has been chosen to represent one of the models of personnel management. Apart from changing the names of the companies, and of the principal characters, the information is accurate. They are small to medium-sized British companies, but the lessons we wish to draw could as easily be found in larger multinationals.

Case study – Epicurus Rentals Limited

This case study is about events which happened at the beginning of 1982. Epicurus Rentals is a television rental company, and is part of the Epicurus Leisure Group. This large British-owned group employs 9000 people throughout the leisure and entertainment fields. These include catering, leisure and sports centres, bingo halls, a television production company, as well as the rental company which has over one million subscribers. The Group's main period of growth was from the mid 1960s to the late 1970s. In the last five years growth has slowed down, and at the time our case is set, there have been no significant recent acquisitions. The Group has come to rely on the rental company for 60% of its turnover.

In the rental company, the only major developments have been the decisions to rent and service micros as part of an initiative by the rental company to move into the home computer market, and the rental of video recorders. The turnover of the rental company is £113 million per

Figure 3   *Organization chart – Epicurus Rentals Ltd*

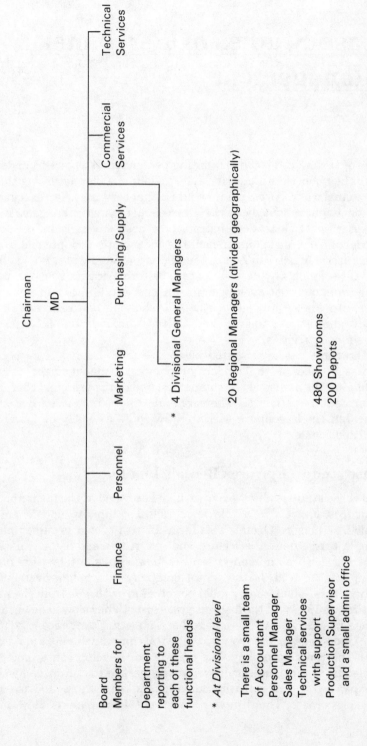

Chairman

MD

Finance   Personnel   Marketing   Purchasing/Supply   Commercial Services   Technical Services

Board
Members for

Department
reporting to
each of these
functional heads

* *At Divisional level*

There is a small team
of Accountant
Personnel Manager
Sales Manager
Technical services
    with support
Production Supervisor
and a small admin office

*   4 Divisional General Managers

20 Regional Managers (divided geographically)

480 Showrooms
200 Depots

annum. The TV rental company is represented throughout the UK with a network of 480 showrooms, (mostly small, but on prime sites), 200 servicing depots and a total staff of 5000 people. There are 2000 technicians, 800 representatives, 450 showroom managers, 200 district and regional managers and 400 staff at head office, as well as cleaners, drivers, storemen etc. Each of the divisions has its own personnel and finance staff, and a divisional sales team with clerical backup services.

The company was reorganized two years ago. The Chairman of Epicurus Rentals is the Chairman of the Epicurus Group and the MD of the rental company is a member of the Group's Board. The structure is shown in Figure 3.

The personnel department

There is a highly organized personnel department at the HQ of the rental company, with representation on the Board of Directors. The department operates comprehensive systems in each of the main areas of personnel management. Detailed policy documents are contained in a large policy manual, which is kept up to date by the HQ personnel staff. There are common conditions of service across the Epicurus Group for pensions, life assurance and senior management conditions. The training staff produce all their own material, and run a large range of programmes for all grades of staff.

Of the technicians 85% are members of the EPTU and 49% of the remaining staff are members of other unions, mostly the EESA. Relationships with management are very good. There are formal procedures for disputes, grievances and discipline to which both management and unions are committed. There was one strike over pay about ten years ago, but since then the technicians in particular have been satisfied with their pay and conditions. There is an annual pay award negotiated to take effect on 1 July every year.

The staff in personnel spend a substantial proportion of their time running and monitoring the systems. They produce reports of their activity frequently, which are incorporated into the annual personnel report for the Board. The data is collected from line management and from the large number of returns required by the personnel department.

The topics covered in the report are consistent with the Personnel Director's main concerns and the areas he brings forward at Board Meetings. The headings covered are:

Number employed	(by grade, occupation, length of service)
Labour turnover	(by grade, occupation, length of service)
Accidents	Time lost, number, etc.
Disputes	Time lost, plus a narrative account of their cause
Grievance procedure	Numbers involved; length of time before complainant had seen appropriate level of management

Discipline procedure	Number who had received warnings etc
Recruitment	Numbers appointed, mean length of time to fill vacancy
Welfare	Expenditure, narrative account of particular problem areas (no names)
Ratios	A series of ratios such as

$$\frac{\text{Training budget}}{\text{Total personnel budget}} \ \%$$

$$\frac{\text{Actual training costs}}{\text{Training budget}} \ \%$$

The Personnel Director defines his role as that of a professional personnel manager, with a thorough understanding of the whole range of personnel techniques. There are regular meetings of Divisional Personnel Managers and HQ personnel staff, and an extensive network of communication between them.

From this description we may conclude that this is a highly organized 'professional' personnel function. It fits closely the 'contracts manager' model in its concentration on systems and techniques. The large personnel hierarchy is devoted to the maintenance of the systems. Such an approach was developed to cope with the spread of managerial authority and the felt need by the headquarters for control. No doubt the personnel department served this need very well.

An orderly change in the product base was anticipated, the corporate plan proposed that the company would remain and develop within the home entertainment field – TV, video, video games, cassettes rental, and would simultaneously develop the renting and servicing of home computers.

The company forecast that changes in the marketing environment, such as greater reliability and easier servicing of the later models, would gradually make inroads into the subscriber list.

The proposed net profit figures in the five-year plan were as follows:

1981/82	1982/83	1983/84	1984/85	1986/87
£25m	£20m	£18m	£24m	£47m

These forecasts were founded on the assumption that the rental of TVs would fall steadily until 1983/84, even with the marketing initiatives (for example, capturing more of the contract rental market in hotels, encouraging rental of second TVs, etc.) but that there would be a steady increase in the rental of video equipment to take up the shortfall. The figures also represented a modest growth in the field of home computers although it was estimated that they would remain a minor contributor for the next five years.

The 'new reality' of 1982

Due to a number of factors, the outcome was rather different from the plan. The 'new reality' of 1982 meant that there would be no steady move to new products, while the company remained profitable. The problems were immediate:

1 The trend towards owning rather than renting accelerated.
2 The recession forced more terminations of rental agreements in areas of high unemployment.
3 The video 'boom' in rental was projected at a time when supplies were difficult and demand was growing. Demand did not increase as projected, and a number of Japanese manufacturers started dumping cheaper videos on the market, thus encouraging purchase.
4 Costs rose sharply, for example the rates on premises, staff costs and distribution costs.

As a result, the projection for 1982/83 was zero net profit.

The Personnel Director, as a member of the Rentals Board, was immediately involved in a series of crisis meetings which attempted to produce a plan for recovery.

Corporate planning had always been led by marketing, and the plan itself was largely financial. Although overall objectives and goals were described, the personnel strategies aimed at achieving these goals were assumed. The company had been largely 'one product', stable and profitable – there seemed no reason to believe that a system which had worked in the past would not be as successful in the future.

If we take the classic 'strategic planning' process, one might expect five distinct steps:

1 Definition of corporate philosophy – what kind of business do we want to be? How do we want to be regarded by customers, employees, and the other stakeholders in society?
2 Environmental conditions are scanned – what is likely to happen, for example, in government policy, unemployment, interest rates, inflation, and in the appropriate industrial sector?
3 Evaluation of corporate strengths and constraints. This involves a 'SWOT' (strengths, weaknesses, opportunities, threats) analysis of the company. The 'strengths and weaknesses' are usually internal, the 'opportunities and threats' external to the company.
4 Objectives and goals emerge from the three stages above, answering the question what business are we in, what should we be in.
5 Strategies are developed to meet these objectives.

Epicurus failed to progress through steps 1 and 2, and had taken steps 3 and 4 together. There had been no involvement of the personnel function, except in the most minimal sense of being informed of the outcome to the process.

The notion that there were personnel strengths and weaknesses which could be exploited, or should be obviated, had not been put to the test before. The personnel function was actively involved in the annual budget procedures, and in explaining budgetary variances, but planning beyond a one-year forecast was anathema to personnel.

In this situation, the Personnel Director found himself with no arguments, no perspective in which to judge the various proposals now proffered in the crisis. He was aware that there should be nothing done in the short term which would prejudice the long term, but what was the long term to be? How could he argue for caution on redundancies, when he had no basis on which to forecast requirements? The panoply of measures with which he had defended his function in the past – accident statistics, costs of training, etc. seemed irrelevant now. The company's human resources were perhaps its greatest strength. In a sense this is a tribute to the benefit of a 'contracts manager' model, which has placed relationships at the centre of reality, based on an assumption of market stability, but how could that strength be mobilized in the face of threats to the major product of the company?

If one views the link between corporate and human resource planning as follows:

Level:	Strategic	Operational	Budget
	Long range (5 years +)	(Over 1 year, under 5 years)	Annual (next year)
	Environment, philosophy SWOT	Forecasting requirements	Action plans

then the Personnel Director has spent his personnel apprenticeship at the budgetary, and to some degree at the operational, level. The personnel director and his personnel staff had seen the necessity to justify the work of the personnel department but in Epicurus, the prevailing orthodoxy dictated a range of efficiency measures, as the normal way to assess the contribution of a headquarters department. The question of what can the personnel department do for the business was not asked, therefore, until the company's markets began to collapse. His problem was therefore how to turn the personnel function from its 'contract manager' mode into an 'architect' mode – to plan change and to act as a high level consultant during the phases of the change programme.

Case study – Thomas Nestor Limited (printers)

This old established book printers was originally a family business. After the London blitz, the company moved from the East End of London to a new location deep in the countryside of England. The company grew and prospered. There were a number of moves to diversify its interests, so that by the end of the 1970s, Nestors included a printers in Singapore, colour printing, book binding, and a large paperback printing works. The old family business had become a 'Group', but was still run by the Nestor family, with a small London registered office, the main positions in the Board being filled by sons of the old chairman.

In the aftermath of the recession Nestors had their investments spread widely, and with inadequate returns from most of their small businesses. The major rethink of their corporate plans which followed was accompanied by a 'night of the long knives' in the boardroom. Facing the realities of the 1980s, a younger board was appointed and the company was restructured. Only one of the old Nestor family remained as a director. The less profitable parts of the company which specialized in colour printing and 'coffee table' books were closed, and new techniques for the production of paperbacks on long runs enabled the company to produce at an economic rate for the mass market. To achieve the economies on their operations which were judged necessary for survival, approximately 600 people were made redundant, leaving a total of 1200 people spread among the remaining parts of the company. In the reorganization, managers were converted to the principles of profit centres. They became accountable for their own units, and a major 'hearts and minds' campaign was undertaken with the workforce, all of whom were members of print trade unions.

As a part of the reorganization, a Personnel Director was appointed, who also had Board responsibility for one of the operating companies. He kept on the elderly, and rather ineffective, personnel manager John Criddle who was relegated to routine personnel administration, recruitment, safety, health and the maintenance of the agreements with the trade unions. Criddle was not a 'professionally' qualified personnel manager, but had joined the company after leaving the Royal Navy. Indeed, his selection procedures still consisted largely of looking at a candidate and then determining whether or not 'he liked the cut of his jib'.

Increasingly Criddle came to be regarded as 'the old retainer'. The company would not fire him because of his years of loyal service, and because he was efficient at performing work of a routine nature; but his style of the 'clerk of works' personnel approach was not in tune with the 'architect' mode preferred by the Personnel Director.

The Personnel Director was indeed one of the chief architects of the new style Nestor Group. Although not a young man, his careful personalized touch and his background of consultancy and training enabled him to develop a strategy of working *with* the unions at the local level. With the aid of the young, dynamic General Manager, the local fathers of the chapel supported the changes at Nestors, even those which entailed their fellow union members removing restrictive practices, and allowing redundancies without disruption. Above all, the Personnel Director did not allow the industrial relations tradition to overwhelm management.

By emphasizing the involvement of the unions in the organization's long-term plans, and by instituting communication techniques for a parallel communication route to the shopfloor, instead of through union meetings, the pressure for greater efficiency was sustained.

A new bonus scheme was introduced, based on the output of each accountable profit centre. This was intended to convey a sense of the organization's purpose and to involve employees directly in the achievements of the company. Managers placed themselves in the position of being answerable to their own unit for their performance, and thus found themselves explaining and discussing their intentions on a detailed basis with their workers.

With the new structure came new roles, and new challenges for management. These were reinforced by the 'new' open style. In order to support the management team and to encourage the general acceptance of the preferred style, a large-scale management development programme was created. In addition to spreading a common management philosophy, and convincing new supervisors and managers of the value of the new articles of faith, the programme was aimed at building the confidence of managers and at imparting a range of managerial skills. A modular approach was taken, spreading the training over 18 months, linking the techniques training in with business planning, and with projects undertaken locally. All supervisors and managers, up to and including the directors participated.

As a consequence of the strategy, relationships throughout the organization were good, even under the strain of redundancies. The communication measures outlined above encouraged involvement in decision-making and resulted in an extremely flexible workforce. Managers 'grew' in stature, became better able to delegate, to solve problems for themselves, and to coordinate and control their units effectively. In the course of a year, a substantial loss was turned around into a £1 million profit.

We can summarize the features of the 'architect' mode we have described in Thomas Nestor.

1   There was a strong business orientation to the personnel function.
2   The personnel function was committed to helping the organization to adapt and to change.
3   There was a close affinity between the personnel policies – a coherent management philosophy was being sold to workpeople backed by deeds as well as words.

Assessment in Thomas Nestor was over the whole compass of personnel policies, which were judged on their contribution to the business. The basic questions, how effective are the training, reward and industrial relations policies for example, had to be answered by their relevance to the business's objectives. It is conceivable that under an architect model personnel department, there is a lack of attention to a detailed systematic assessment of the efficiency of personnel policies, since the costs of measuring efficiency would need also to be justified by the same business criteria. There would be an awareness of the main costs and benefits of each policy initiated, however.

In the two cases we have presented so far, we have described examples of the 'contracts manager' and of the 'architect' models. The 'contracts manager' model in particular seems vulnerable to the difficulties of assessment. The problems of assessing the contribution of personnel management to the business are well illustrated by the case that follows, in which we can demonstrate how the issue of evaluation can become enmeshed in the 'political' processes within the company.

Case study – Archon Engineering Group

This was a British owned engineering and chemicals group in the early 1970s. The formal organization chart for senior staff is shown in Figure 4.

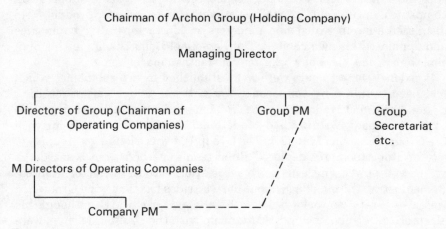

Figure 4

The Chairman of the Archon Group, an ageing knight, had been invited to take on the office, after a brief spell as a part-time director. Instead of behaving as a figurehead, as had been anticipated by his fellow directors, he began a series of moves to establish his power. First of all he shifted the existing managing director into a lucrative overseas post in a subsidiary, then arranged for the appointment of a new young MD from outside, whom he regarded as his voice in the executive councils of the enterprise. By a number of moves he was able to remove the few remaining old members of the family which had founded Archon in the 1920s, who had independent means and were a rival source of power.

The prevailing managerial ethos was upper middle class. Directors under the old regime had typically been the product of public schools and Oxbridge. The new Chairman and his supporters came from the same stable, but in addition to the continuation of this management ideology, they wanted to see an overlay of professionalism. In practice this meant that managers were expected to drop the pose of the gifted amateur, and instead to display commitment, interest and a slick gloss to their speech and actions. With this change in management style came a greater centralization of services, and a move to concentrate the business more in the area of engineering, factory control systems and services for the oil industry, and away from chemicals and consumer products. There was no formal corporate plan. Broad financial targets were set over a five-year period, but were varied annually according to marketing projections. There was no explicit statement at this time about the future of the operating companies.

The MDs of operating companies reported through holding company directors. The changes brought about by the new Chairman therefore had a profound effect. One of the supporters of the Chairman on the Board, Alexander Robertson, was made responsible for a 'division' of operating companies, in the fields of chemicals, paints and consumer products. He dismissed a number of senior managers within the operating companies and appointed his own choices. The Personnel Departments in this division were of the 'clerk of works' or 'contracts manager' type.

Personnel Departments were well established in two companies which had been acquired by the Group, where trade unions had negotiating rights. Personnel Managers in the division reported on a day-to-day basis to their company MDs but had a functional 'dotted-line' relationship with the Group Personnel Manager. The Group PM was a long-time, if uneasy, ally of Robertson. He deplored Robertson's methods, but wanted the status and power which his close association with the Director granted. Remembering the old adage about 'he who rides the tiger', the Group PM was also careful to make links with the new Group MD, although his attempts of forming a closer relationship with the Group Chairman were rejected.

Robertson's view of personnel management was as a low grade operational necessity which could be used on occasions as a control on operating companies, or as an agent of change to further his own aims. Thus, operating company personnel managers became involved with the introduction of new procedures and the Group Personnel Manager busied himself with the creation of formal, group-wide personnel policies. After several abortive attempts at a general agreement on his proposals the Group PM resorted to working privately, putting his drafts to Robertson and the Group MD before issuing them as agreed statements of policy. The difficulties this caused at a local level were largely ignored, or left to individual personnel managers to cope with by putting a case for variation to the Group PM. As the companies in the Group operated within different industries, with different industrial relations traditions, many of the new central policies were treated as 'dead letters' for as long as possible. The assessment of all personnel activity in the Consumer Products Division was, therefore, against this 'political' background.

The criteria for the success of any personnel action in this Division of the Group could be listed as follows:

1 How did it support Robertson? In particular, what did the action contribute to the centralization of operations, or to the build-up of those parts of the business favoured by the Group Chairman and MD? This could only be guessed.
2 To what extent did it fit in with operating company MDs' plans? MDs had only outline plans, and annual budgets.
3 Did the action represent the Personnel Department in a way which Robertson would find acceptable? (For example, if it was a really good idea, it had to be seen as emanating jointly from Personnel and the senior line manager.)
4 Was the work conducted with an appropriate style or 'flair' – with some risk-taking, plus a glossy verbal or written report of activities, showing how good the whole conduct of the work had been?

The way ahead for an operating company Personnel Manager may seem obvious. After all, if he cleared his plans with his immediate superior, the MD of the Unit, what difficulties for him could there be? Clarity was often difficult to find, however. The MDs were unsure of Robertson's stand on some issues. For example, Robertson was not prepared to say what should be done about research and development. Thus, even if there was ostensibly a vacancy for a development engineer, it might be unwise to fill the vacancy too quickly. If a MD sought clarification he would be advised to use his own judgement; the decision would consequently reflect on him personally if a problem occurred later. Too many 'problems' at a later date could be said to reflect on the unit MD's judgement in general. Of course, what was defined as a problem ex post facto was in itself dependent on Robertson and the Group Chairman.

In this environment, assessment by superiors and peers was on a basis of personality and behaviour within the management team. The formation of alliances, preferably with powerful figures, was one way of ensuring that one's work was defined as successful. This did not mean that mistakes were easily forgiven. If there were obvious errors, it would be difficult for the personnel manager to form an alliance next time, and his isolation would make him vulnerable. Those who did not bother to seek allies, or to trade benefits with line manager colleagues, might still find approval as 'risk takers', if they were palpably successful. To adopt such an approach was to live dangerously, however, and such a person would be an easy prey for other members of the team to destroy, for instance, if expenditure rose well beyond budget levels. In the political arena, 'fall guys' are essential. Where assessment is based on personality, failure must be attributable to an individual and until the person can be identified, all are under threat.

Whatever the formal status of the personnel executive, without the depth of knowledge, experience and managerial skills there will be difficulty in demonstrating competence. Personnel practitioners must operate within the organization's socio-political system, and to neglect survival skills results in the assumption by the assessors that the personnel department has nothing to offer.

Summary

In the Epicurus case, the Personnel Director had established techniques for measuring the efficiency of his department, but until the collapse of the market he had not understood the importance of relating the efficiency of his department to the corporate objectives of the business. At a time of stability, the 'contracts manager' model provided for an attractive organizational society in which to live and work, a society where efficiency needs were well-measured, but where the effectiveness of the personnel function was never considered. By contrast, the personnel director in Thomas Nestor was primarily concerned with the achievement of business objectives. For him, the effectiveness of the personnel function could clearly be assessed by measuring the extent to which it had achieved these objectives. In the case of the Archon Group, the Group Personnel Manager was enmeshed in political intrigue because he was unable to interpret the model of personnel suitable for his organization. He lacked the skills to be able to separate out clear personnel objectives which were related to the objectives of the business, and to gain support for achieving them.

We therefore see a distinction between effectiveness and technical efficiency. Effectiveness is assessed by measuring achievement of personnel management objectives that are functional for the business; that is, those which correspond to the roles we discussed in Chapter 3.

In Table 1, under each personnel objective, we have entered the typical objectives with which the function is concerned. Under the techniques heading we show methods and measurements on which the achievement of objectives could be assessed, and our skills column summarizes those skills where competence is required in order to operate the techniques successfully. Efficiency is assessed by measuring the costs of applying personnel techniques. Skills and techniques require a knowledge of social science and of business management. The principal skills required of personnel managers, on which they are assessed, are when and how to apply the techniques, and how to sell their services to client line managers, and top executives.

Table 1 shows the relative position of the roles, objectives, techniques and skills we have been discussing.

Effectiveness		*Technical efficiency (examples)*	
Functional roles	*Typical personnel objectives*	*Techniques*	*Skills*
Adapt to environment	Manage change	Organization development ER strategies Job redesign Planning, co-ordinating	Inter-personal Social Consultancy
Goal attainment	Business objectives expressed as specific tasks	Budget control ratios (from corporate plan) Planning, organizing	Financial Business management Decision-making
Integrate	Core values implied in policies	Employee relations strategies Organization design	Communication Persuasion Negotiation
Maintain roles	Personnel systems agreed with line management	Management of internal labour markets	Interpersonnel Statistical/ administrative

6
Assessing the Effectiveness of Personnel Management

This chapter will explore the issues and problems of assessing the *effectiveness* of the personnel function as a whole, rather than its technical efficiency or the effectiveness of particular policies. We can define the personnel function's 'effectiveness' as the extent to which the members of the personnel department, and the personnel policies give effect to the organization's objectives. Thus the issue of how much the policies cost is relevant only if these costs form part of the organization's objectives.

There are a number of immediate problems we must deal with as a consequence of defining personnel effectiveness. Firstly, the objectives that one might expect a company to possess are frequently not agreed in detail, or in some cases, discussed at all. While one might anticipate the corporate plan to contain organizational objectives, these may only be set out in the broadest possible terms. In many instances, there will be no corporate plans, even if there are short-term financial and sales plans and budgets. Where there are broad plans, there may be no attempt to derive measurable or even recognizable objectives from the long term 'strategy'.

Even where there are formal objectives, and plans to achieve them, circumstances may change so rapidly (changes to competitors, new technology, inflation, for example can change plans dramatically) that the objectives of a year ago become obsolete. It would not be unusual for groups of managers either to be following their own plans, or to be adopting plans which, if achieved, would negate the efforts of their colleagues. For example, profitability in the short term may be incompatible with growth in the long term. The traditional 'enmity' between sales and production led in the case of one company to an increase in sales being projected while the production director was trying to introduce new equipment and working methods, with delays and quality problems arising as orders increased.

The personnel department is more likely to be vague about the personnel policy objectives because achievement in such areas as recruitment, industrial relations, employee appraisal and management development is difficult to measure. We can thus see that there are a number of major problems in the assessment process which limit the possibilities of discovering satisfactory assessment methods. These might be put as a series of questions. For example, does an organization articulate what it wants? Are the goals clearly set, enabling achievement and effectiveness to be fairly assessed? Is there a unitary set of expectations, or are there different expectations being voiced by clients almost to, or perhaps beyond, any point of reconciliation? In what dimensions and in what ways is a personnel function expected to be effective?

One of the first difficulties we encounter when answering these questions is the problem of assessing any managerial job. Managerial work tends to be difficult to assess because the end product is in someone else's labour. Here we may recall Bertrand Russell's slightly mischievous explanation:

> Work is of two kinds: first, altering the position of matter at or near the earth's surface relatively to other such matter; second telling other people to do so. The first kind is unpleasant and ill paid; the second is pleasant and highly paid. The second kind is capable of indefinite extension: there are not only those who give orders, but those who give advice as to what orders should be given.[1]

Personnel work, as organizational work, is part of that class of activities which is capable of extension into ever higher orders of administration.[2] For example, in evaluating the efficiency with which the personnel department established an appraisal system, we are assessing the effectiveness of the personnel department's methods of assessment. The argument here is not an elaborate sophistry. There has grown a whole level of administration where the activity of managers is so remote from risk-bearing action that it is not possible to assess their work by showing any directly related adjustment to revenue, profit or costs as a consequence of their behaviour. We have already considered the organizational roles of personnel when we described how the personnel function serves to represent the central value system of the organization, to maintain the organization's boundaries, to provide stability and continuity, and to adapt the organization to change. Three main areas where effectiveness may be judged spring from these organizational roles. The effectiveness of personnel management will be considered in this chapter, under these headings:

1   At the individual level of the personnel practitioner;
2   At the level of the role and relationships with those in the same employment network; and
3   In the wider context of the personnel function's contribution to the strategic development of the organization.

The effective individual practitioner

There are no 'scientific' or objective measures of senior managers' work. Their deeds are always coloured by the 'political' groupings, the cross-cutting alliances and cliques through which power is sought and exercised.[3] Relationships are crucial for most managers, and thus their own personality is a factor in performance. One answer to the question of the basis for assessment is therefore to look at how behaviour in the management team is assessed.

There is a strong argument in favour of assessing the performance of personnel managers by assessing their interpersonal behaviour. Performance in the management team is very dependent on relationships between the team members. Good communication between team members is vitally important, and this includes the capacity to give and receive feedback from colleagues. The behaviours of managers as individuals relating to their subordinates and to the people they wish to influence are crucial. A persistently disruptive or confrontive style harms relationships, delays the completion of business, and is inimical to discussion. Personnel managers, often without formal authority, have a need to influence manager colleagues and work people in order to sustain personnel policies, to motivate others and to control personnel systems.

It would seem reasonable, therefore, to assess personnel managers by the influence of their personality on others. Clearly the ebullient, attractive person would seem to have immediate advantages, but few senior managers are so naive that they do not go beyond first impressions. The extrovert may prove irresponsible, or find it difficult to say 'no'. The introvert may be highly regarded as 'solid' or 'conscientious'. When assessing their colleagues managers are assessing the influence rather than the character of the person concerned. Typically, such assessment is by informal means: quiet discussions after meetings comparing notes, a few words on the telephone with interested parties, the 'grapevine', and observations of behaviour are well tried methods. Such methods are not 'objective', but they are rational, in that whether or not a personnel manager is highly regarded by colleagues is one important criterion for successful performance.

However, there are disadvantages in such an informal approach to assessment. The management team may be too cosy in its relationships. The 'don't rock the boat' syndrome can be a sign of fear of exposure to change, or to sharper wits. Our all-pervading class structure creates 'halo' and 'cloven hoof' effects – 'He must be all right, he went to Cambridge' or 'His accent lets him down. . .' are statements which betray tribal loyalties rather than a rational assessment of value. Perhaps the most insidious distortion provided by these informal methods is where managers are mutually benevolent in their assessments of each other for the purposes of sustaining a useful alliance with a colleague, or in return for a favour: 'He helped me, so I'm going to say he's OK.' Senior managers who have helped to recruit the personnel manager, or have recommended the individual for promotion may be reluctant to admit their mistakes in spite of contrary evidence.

The personnel manager being assessed is not a passive bystander during the process of assessment. To be an organization survivor one needs quickly to discover the local success criteria. An early success is usually helpful in establishing a favourable reputation. One might expect an effort to create a good impression at meetings, and with the boss, early on in the relationship. It would be consistent with such a carefully orchestrated plan for the manager to seek out those activities that have a high visibility in the organization, and then to concentrate on them. If he or she can be associated with a high status activity, so much the better. The range of tactics for making out in a new job could be elaborated, but we have shown by these illustrations how the assessment process becomes enmeshed with the political ploys acted out in the organization, when assessment rests on behaviour and personality.

Nevertheless, whatever other measures of performance are used, the assessment of personality and behaviour remain central to the judgement of managerial ability. Personnel managers would seem to be particularly suitable for this type of assessment, because of their place in the organization's central value system, and since their work is so concerned with the management of relationships. This informal 'trial by peers' type of assessment is therefore inevitable. The particular form it takes is contingent upon a range of factors, including the size, structure, traditions and the history of the enterprise.

The failure so often ascribed to human resource specialists to make a major contribution to the corporate plan is due to both structural reasons and a lack of individual effectiveness. Informal and formal means are needed to influence management decision-making. To make a contribution, it is necessary for the human resource specialist to belong to the organization's dominant coalition – the inner circle of top management who take the strategic decisions, and who represent strong values about the organization. Gaining access to the decision-making forum, the Board or management meetings is one aspect, but the other informal processes are also significant, especially selling personnel ideas to department heads, or to other powerful figures. This can sometimes be achieved by incorporating their ideas and their criticisms of existing arrangements into the plans, and giving them a sense of ownership.

From this analysis we may say that effectiveness in management is attributed to those who appear able to control the work environment, and that effectiveness at the personal level springs from the self-confidence this achievement brings.[4] We have already indicated that to be sustained this kind of personal effectiveness must go beyond mere presentation skills, or political manoeuvring; a broad knowledge of general management, plus personnel techniques and their theoretical base in the social sciences underpin the interpersonal skills of personnel work. When personnel specialists seek to be involved in corporate planning they move into territory which marketing and financial managers have long regarded as their own. Machiavelli's words should be heeded:

The desire to acquire territory is a very common and natural thing; and when a man who is capable of doing it makes the attempt, he will generally be praised, or at least not blamed: the error and blame arise when a man lacks the necessary ability and still wants to make the attempt at all costs.[5]

Effective personnel roles

The three models we have described give personnel specialists different roles by sustaining different expectations about the purposes and functions of specialist personnel management. Each model therefore represents a different kind of effectiveness.

Clerk of works This is a resource acquisition view of effectiveness. The evaluation is based on the contribution to the organization's inputs: recruitment, quality of personnel appointed, the way the department serves management needs, measured by the speed and cost of the service.

Contracts manager This is an organizational efficiency model of effectiveness, where the throughput is evaluated by reference to the maintenance of productive relationships through personnel systems. The effectiveness of training and productivity measures are most likely to be used under this model.

Architect This is a goal attainment model of effectiveness, where the effectiveness of the department is judged entirely by its impact on the organization's output. The creative management of the internal labour market, and its interaction with the environment will be seen as the sphere where judgements are made. The measurement of the results as defined in the corporate plan provide a straightforward basis for assessing whether the management of the effort/reward bargains struck has been successful.

In dealing with the question of whether an organization articulates its personnel requirements, we must also recall that both the time frame for results to appear, and the role of the people making the evaluation are important.

For many types of managerial work, the long time lapse before results can be evaluated makes assessment problematic. The time span over which the personnel function's decisions can be evaluated divides into three periods dependent on the type of activity.

There are immediate, short-term decisions which would typically concern the organization of work, overcoming staff shortages, employee grievances and similar day-to-day activities. Feedback on these areas is rapid.

In the mid-term range of one to two years, decisions about recruitment, training, organization planning, and the substantive agreements with trade unions can be judged for their efficiency. This time frame allows a mature appreciation of whether a suitable person was appointed, the utility of a training course, and how economic a wage bargain was seen to be.

It is in the assessment of those decisions that have a long-term pay-off that the greatest problem arises. Taking a period of five years or more, corporate planning decisions with their human resource implications will be far too distant to be reviewed in the light of the results. In any planning process, there is a re-evaluation of objectives as a consequence of changing conditions and subsequent amendments will lead to incremental adjustments to personnel policies. Indeed, personnel policy often evolves in response to changing conditions, and discrete steps are not always visible. With changing objectives it is difficult to weigh the outcomes against the original aims. In the case of some activities, for example an industrial relations strategy, or a management development programme, it may be undesirable to formulate precise objectives. Industrial relations strategies have varying possible outcomes and the long-term development of people is often perceived as an act of faith in the future. What is considered effective performance is a factor in relation to which model of personnel management predominates. Frustrating as it undoubtedly is, effectiveness is a relative concept dependent on general organization standards of performance and on the personnel model which governs personnel activity in the organization.

The adept and persuasive personnel specialist can bring a particular model into being searching always for congruity with the organization's expectations. We see this as a definition of effectiveness in personnel management. Judgements of effectiveness will start from an assessment of whether the function reflects the broad aspirations and goals of the assessor. Judgements on efficiency start from an assessment as to how efficiently the function performs against a matrix of performance criteria which will not be dissimilar to those generally employed by the organization for all functions.

A clear understanding by personnel specialists that options exist, that analytically different models of personnel management can be brought into being is often missing from their professional perceptions. They are not without choices, not unarmed in the face of line management calls for a different approach to personnel management, not defenceless when hearing a call from a chief executive for a more effective personnel department.

We discussed the differences between assessors in Chapter 4, when we suggested that the assessors fall into two groups. There are those who

share the same web of employment relationships as the personnel specialists and those who live outside the web.

Among the most important assessors is the chief executive. Few personnel departments are so fortunate as to have from their chief executive
as clear a mandate as that offered by Sir Michael Edwardes writing in
March 1983:

> The welfare of the company's employees is first and foremost a function of
> the company's profitability and survival. The role of the personnel manager
> is to promote that profitability by the most effective management of the
> company's total human resource.[6]

Others within the web of employee relationships include the top management team, senior line management, and other personnel specialists. Perhaps the most underrated assessors are the employees themselves. We
would also recall that trade union officials, suppliers and customers
assess personnel from outside the employment relationship.

To discover how personnel specialists thought they were evaluated, we
asked 20 experienced personnel specialists from public and private sector
organizations to describe how from their experience, they were evaluated
by the Board, by line managers, and by themselves.[7]

1 Board criteria: Personnel specialists should
   - be able to sell themselves to management;
   - have an appreciation of the business;
   - control personnel costs; and
   - create high quality manpower resources.

2 Line managers: Personnel specialists should
   - have the ability to solve line managers' personnel problems;
   - be judged by the speed and quality of their communications;
   - be available;
   - be visible; and
   - be judged on the accuracy of their advice.

3 Personnel specialists' judgement of their own effectiveness:
   personnel specialists should
   - be judged by their satisfaction of client demands;
   - by achievement of specific objectives;
   - by involvement in central policy-making;
   - be satisfied by seeing their ideas implemented; and
   - anticipate needs of their clients.

From this list one may deduce that the personnel specialists' version of
effectiveness is not very different from what one might expect of all
managers. The consultancy role, together with all the skills associated
with influencing others without direct authority, emerges as the key role
that they must fulfill well to be effective. This still leaves the question
of how employees on the whole assess personnel management. These

evaluations are possibly not prominent for personnel specialists but are inferred from the other measures.

One difficulty experienced by the personnel specialist, reaching for congruity between management expectations, and the model of personnel which seems appropriate, is the frequent absence of any rational judgement about the role of personnel. In the Archon case, for example, Robertson had a jaundiced view of personnel work throughout his career. Senior managers who are not disposed to search for the personnel function's contribution, may assume it contributes nothing. The difficulties inherent in the assessment process add to the problem, and questions about how much power personnel staff were given to solve problems are often not asked.

In some companies, a management by exception approach is taken where the assumption is made that when no problems have appeared the personnel department must be working at a satisfactory level of performance. Although there are benefits from a management by exception approach, where delegation and trust are encouraged, management by exception can paradoxically result in only the difficulties and mistakes being discussed, with insufficient praise for the successful completion of everyday tasks.

The problems arise from the frequently incorrect inferences that are drawn when assumptions about performance are made. Profit is a function of a complex of variables, including competitors' actions, government regulations, interest rates and consumer fashions, as well as managerial ability. Blue chip companies are not completely manned by successful, energetic, clever people nor is 'Carey Street' populated by duffers. Assessment based on company performance does not distinguish the effective from the ineffective manager.

The problem of introducing new models of personnel is the problem of changing expectations. As we have indicated, one does not normally start from a neutral base, since line management and board members already have a view based on assumptions about performance. The key to linking the internal processes, that is the personnel policies, to the changing environment in which the organization operates is in the role and relationships of the personnel department. When trying to change an organization, the strategic planner is caught between the internal capabilities of the organization, and the changes in the external environment.[8]

We have argued that the effectiveness of the personnel role can be judged by the department's capacity to bring into being a model of personnel work which meets the needs of the organization, and which thus helps to structure the expectations and relationships of the department's clients.

The strategic development of the organization

For the personnel department to be effective, it must make a contribution to the strategic development of the organization. The major policy decisions, in the fields of employee relations, recruitment, training, development, and reward structures, offer the opportunity to advise on strategic choices where there is a personnel function operating in the 'contracts manager' or the 'architect' mode.

One of the difficulties experienced by those seeking to influence strategic thinking in this area is the frequent absence of an 'employment policy'. For many British companies, personnel policies each stand alone, and unlike the Germans or Japanese, no coherent philosophy of management is promulgated. An employment policy has been defined as:

> an overall employment strategy which integrates the organization's various personnel policies and manpower plans. It should enable it to meet and absorb the changing requirements of technology and markets in the foreseeable future.[9]

In addition to the procedure and substantive agreements on terms and conditions, the manpower policies covering careers, part-time and full-time employment issues and the company's stance on employee involvement might also be expected to form a part of the company's employment policy.

To illustrate the way personnel policies interact, we will take three types of recruitment policy. Each of these policies will result in different approaches to careers, to rewards, to management development, and will result in significantly different organization cultures.

In each of these examples, different approaches to personnel management are required. In cases 1 and 2 the personnel department, or its equivalent, has to manage the internal labour market through a form of soft contracting, whereas in case 3 no such management is required (i.e. no appraisal, promotion or career structure). Case 3 is typical of organizations undergoing rapid change, or uncertain about their future. The personnel department in case 2 requires formalized rules, especially where there are trade unions or house unions (e.g. common interest groups) involved. The two cultures which emerge from case 1 may have significant repercussions on employee relations in general, requiring extra effort in the field of communications and joint consultation to overcome the likely problems. With single tier or two-tier recruitment, there may be a need to bring in specialists to fill particular positions, which means policies have to be developed to help socialize the specialists. Even so, there are particular problems in creating promotion channels for specialists (as exemplified in the British civil service). Multiple recruitment at all levels places an extra strain on the reward structure because of its extreme sensitivity to market rates.

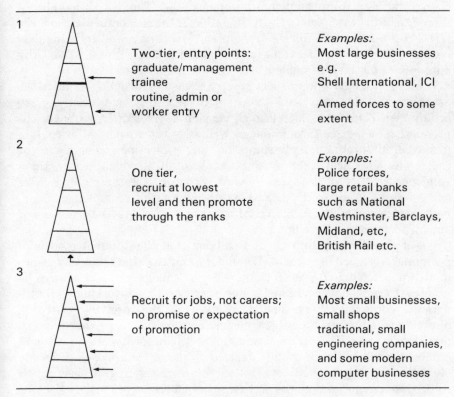

1	Two-tier, entry points: graduate/management trainee routine, admin or worker entry	*Examples:* Most large businesses e.g. Shell International, ICI Armed forces to some extent
2	One tier, recruit at lowest level and then promote through the ranks	*Examples:* Police forces, large retail banks such as National Westminster, Barclays, Midland, etc, British Rail etc.
3	Recruit for jobs, not careers; no promise or expectation of promotion	*Examples:* Most small businesses, small shops traditional, small engineering companies, and some modern computer businesses

To make a significant contribution to the corporate plan, managers must be conscious of the interrelationships between personnel policies and be able to express the relationships in a coherent employment policy. The task of influencing corporate plans is also eased if the organization has strong values about employing people, which can act as a touchstone for decisions. These values need to be understood and operationalized. One of the best examples of a strongly held set of paternalistic values is with Marks and Spencer. Lord Sieff sees this as a managerial, not just a personnel responsibility.[10] Although employing 900 personnel staff out of a total headcount of 50,000 he points out that 'good human relations is not something that can be left to the personnel department'. The senior board 'spend a lot of time on personnel problems' and there is no rigid distinction between line and personnel managers. The strong welfare orientation is a core value, running through the business, and the clarity of view gives corporate personnel policies a coherence. In 1983, Marks and Spencer spent £57 million on catering subsidies, medical and dental care, non-contributory pensions and profit shares. Their pretax profits in 1983/84 were £279 million.

The effectiveness of personnel management is now judged not only on its direct contribution to the corporate plan, but also on the way that the changes arising from the plan are implemented. The distinction should therefore be drawn between the formulation of the corporate plan, and the strategies needed to implement the plan. Strategies need to be double-headed: with both business objectives and societal objectives to be met by appropriate methods of implementation.

The specific contributions personnel can make to formulation are in the assessment of the skills needed now and in the future, and through make or buy type decisions which lead to varying degrees of control over the production or service throughput as well as to the output. All corporate plans contain productivity assumptions and projections on employment costs plus time scales for making changes, all of which depend upon employee relations strategies, reward structures, recruitment policies and training capacities. To make a major contribution to implementation, personnel departments have to confront issues on employee involvement, and on organization development.

We have indicated throughout this book that the different models of personnel work are legitimate. We understand that the opportunities to make major contributions to the process of change may not always be granted to personnel specialists. For example, those working in multi-national companies may find themselves on the receiving end of a directive which gives them little choice. In a recent survey of 30 multi-nationals in the UK, operating budgets, capital investment decisions, and numbers employed were usually decided by parent companies, and wage increases were 'approved' by the parent companies. However, union recognition, negotiations, the settlement of strikes, were mainly decided by the UK subsidiary.[11] This gives the impression that strategic issues are decided by the parent company whereas tactical matters of how to deal with particular problems are handled locally.

Even where there are substantial directives from parent companies, there may still be the opportunity to provide an input to the decision-making process. Managing the changes themselves through the implementation strategies does give scope for assisting the strategic development of the organization. The human resource implications of the corporate plan will be felt in the immediate operating activities of the organization.

By a strange paradox, increased uncertainty in the business environment has given a greater emphasis to corporate planning. In the words of the chairman of one large company, 'Managements have enough problems to face these days without any unwelcome surprises'.[12] Awareness of the need for change, and for responsiveness from management and work-force focuses attention on the human resource. Most managements are aware of the size of the company's investment in people. In one major clothing manufacturer the salary bill for indirect labour constitutes two-thirds of the costs of running the business.

Changes in the economic and social environment that have a direct bearing on the employment of people have heightened interest in the planning of labour requirements. External influences on demand for labour, such as inflation, high interest rates, taxation changes, youth training, Government subsidies, greater competition from overseas, and perhaps most significantly, step changes in new technology bring manning levels into question. There are also important changes in the external labour supply, with more women in the labour force, scarce skills and changes to the size of union membership. However, the greatest impetus to planning usually comes from an awareness of the need to overcome problems with the internal labour supply: redundancy, re-organizations or rapid expansion for example.

In the corporate planning process, the analysis of the company's strengths, weaknesses, opportunities and threats entails the evaluation of personnel implications. Let us consider some illustrations of these personnel consequences. Among the strengths, one may count the reser-voir of expertise in the organization, or the high quality of the employee relationships. Similarly a record of industrial unrest may be perceived as a weakness which results in a substantial amendation to marketing strategy, as was threatened by British Rail in 1982 and British Leyland in the 1983 Cowley dispute.

Productivity levels are an important factor in long-term planning. Here, the organization's reward structure may be utilized tactically, as exemplified by the National Coal Board's bonus scheme. In this case, by introducing a bonus scheme (initially at the least militant pits) the National Coal Board was able to increase output substantially and to build up massive stocks, thus weakening the strike threat for two years. At the same time, the Board followed a policy of selling off its company houses to miners, which together with the higher earnings granted some of the miners a stake in the industry. The long-term 'Plan for Coal' set down the prime requirement of industrial peace. However, there were three strike calls by militant mineworkers' leader Arthur Scargill which were turned down by the miners, before the National Union of Mineworkers was able to bring out the majority of the miners on strike. Even so, those at the Nottinghamshire pits refused the strike call, dividing the union, vindicating the strategy of the former Coal Chief, Lord Ezra.

We can summarize the significance of the human resource implications for the corporate plan by recalling the restraints on operational efficiency caused by failures in planning. These key aspects of the manpower plan are shown in Figure 5.

The management of the change process offers a major role for the per-sonnel function in improving organizational efficiency. For example smoothing the employment curve, or deciding the rate of change in man-power requirements, is extremely important. The choices of when and how many people should be made redundant are not easy.

Costs   ⎫ Productivity assumptions   ⎫ IR implications
        ⎬ Numbers/levels required   ⎬ and reward systems
        ⎭ Scarce skills   ⎫ Recruitment and
                                          training implications
          Management development   ⎫ Implications for
Lead times ⎫ Succession plans   ⎬ future – type of
                                          ⎭ business
          New relationships/
          organization structure   ⎫
                                        ⎬ IR implications
          Kinds of jobs being   ⎭
          created

Figure 5

For example, if a projected downturn is to be short-lived, should the people be retained or should they be dismissed now and recruited at a later date? Should other solutions, such as overtime, sub-contracting or casual labour be considered for the peak requirements?

When British Airways was formed by merging BOAC and BEA, the management hoped to expand their services into the excess capacity they had acquired. The advent of wide-bodied jets, high oil prices and the world recession dramatically changed the business. As a consequence the airline was obliged to shed ten thousand people over five years at a cost in excess of £100 million.[13]

There are therefore social considerations, and the heavy costs of redundancies to avoid. Most organizations relish their good name. To be known as a 'good employer' – that is, to be socially responsible – is important for their image, hence for their ability to raise capital in the City, and such a reputation also increases their chances of obtaining government contracts. Planning alerts management to the likely consequences of following the current policies now, and provides time to avoid any unsatisfactory consequences. Admittedly, there are uncertainties in the future. The planning time horizons are different for different businesses. The longer the time span over which we plan, the greater the uncertainty, and the further ahead we look, the less relevant is our current position.

However, given the possibilities for projecting alternative estimates of the future by using computer applications, predictions are possible. These can use a mixture of factual information derived from lead indicators, and multiple regression on the demand side, and supply side forecasting deriving from the analysis of the organization's manpower systems. Even without the precision of numbers required for actual recruitment to occur, these models can offer alternative scenarios, which may be subject to a sensitivity analysis. In this way, a series of 'what if' questions may be asked, enabling management to consider a range of values arising from different policy options, and to assess the consequences of each variation. Flexibility in manpower controls should emanate from this process, allowing management the chance of revising plans to meet new conditions.

The company image is also important to the people who work for it. The motivational aspects of good planning procedures derive from the confidence people have in the future of the business, and in the ability of management to run it. Good employee relations may require the sharing or involvement of trade unions in the planning process. Indeed in several countries their involvement is mandatory. Creating the right climate for productivity improvement is essential in employee relations. The part played by individual members of the management team may vary with their personalities and power positions. The managing director will inevitably be a major contributor.

This is exemplified by the transformation of Vickers from an ailing engineering company into a high technology company with few of the old 'them and us' attitudes. David Plastow, the MD, has been the prime mover in the change process, leading by example, and with a philosophy of management which he explained in a recent article:

> You have to have the discipline of a soldier, and a surgeon. Apart from the basic numeracy, you must have the ability to identify the task, and match it to the individual. Then it's spending 90 per cent of your time encouraging him, showing you've got confidence in him.[14]

The effectiveness of policies on changes for aggregates of people is often judged by the smoothness of the changes. One of the roles of the personnel function here is to ensure that changes in the demand for manpower are smoothed over time. For example, that sudden fluctuations are smoothed out by sub-contracting, overtime, or redeployment instead of recruitment and dismissal. The level at which the employment curve is angled will be dependent on cost and employee relations considerations. The personnel policy outcomes from the corporate plan derive from the numbers and attributes of the people required, and their cost. These policy outcomes will therefore include redundancy, or 'de-manning', management development, training, recruitment, reward policies, and may reflect changes to the structure of the organization and the rationalization of conditions of service when a new company is acquired.

During the 1960s there was a growth in the use of social science techniques to manage changes in organizations. 'Organization development', or OD as this came to be called, takes a number of forms, depending on the type and depth of intervention. Broadly, a socio-technical systems approach is taken, and so projects are often introduced when there is new technology or some major change of investment. The typical methods for achieving changes in attitudes and commitment include job redesign schemes, ergonomic applications, and a variety of communication techniques and instruments for revealing the facts about roles and relationships.

Lisl Klein distinguishes between a 'bounded' service and a 'diffuse' service.[15] In a bounded service the work is brought to the department, or individual, the problems are defined for the internal or external consultant. In a diffuse service, there are opportunities for the company-wide investigation of issues, and much more autonomy for the consultant. We would anticipate that assessment in the bounded case would be very results-oriented, whereas in the more diffuse role, assessment would be on the process of the consultancy, as much as on the outcome, since one of the purposes of OD is to facilitate organizational learning.

Assessment of achievements from OD schemes is not easily made. When writing a postscript to the large-scale change programme at Shell which was based on an OD approach, Paul Hill pointed to the difficulty of identifying those changes which were attributable to what was called 'the philosophy programme.[16] To attempt to make major changes to a whole philosophy of management in a multinational is an ambitious project, and so perhaps we should not be too critical of the absence of any measurable objectives in the programme. There was no economic yardstick either. However, questionaires sent to departmental managers revealed results covering detailed changes in procedures, jobs, increased personal commitment, and the more noticeable pursuit of company objectives. In spite of an original conception of an annual assessment of the results, only one assessment was made, in 1967.

Organizational politics, which are themselves part of the data on the organization, influence the role of the OD consultant to a point where assessment is subverted, according to Klein's experiences at Esso. She argues that the client has to become more knowledgeable and discriminating about social science to achieve results. The type of intervention she describes of a social scientist attempting to offer relatively 'value-free' advice to a business seems almost an anachronism today.

Summary

For a personnel function to be effective, we have argued that each of the three conditions we have described should be met. Effectiveness must exist at the level of the individual, at the level of the organizational role, and the function must be seen to contribute to the development of the business. Each of these is not a necessary and sufficient condition. Each condition is dependent on the other:

Individual effectiveness → Effective role → Effective contribution
to the development of
the business

We have stressed in this chapter the relationship between the personnel function's activities and the organization's economic purpose. The assessment of the different models of personnel work is different because they operate under different criteria. There is no doubt, however, that the architect model is more concerned than the others with the process of rapid change, and at meeting corporate purposes, even at the expense of societal objectives which seek more democratic and slower approaches to changing people at work, in which the societal stakeholders can be involved.

Notes

1 B. Russell, *In Praise of Idleness* (London: George Allen and Unwin, Unwin paperbacks, 1976), p. 13.

2 R. Jones and C. Lakin, *The Carpetmakers* (Maidenhead: McGraw-Hill, 1978).

3 See, for example, M. Dalton, *Men who Manage* (New York: Wiley, 1959) and C. Sofer, *Men in Mid Career* (Cambridge: Cambridge University Press, 1970).

4 J.J. Morse, 'Sense of competence and individual managerial performance', *Psychological Reports 32* (1976), pp. 1195–8.

5 N. Machiavelli, *The Prince*. Trans. by B. Penman (J.M. Dent, 1981) p. 51.

6 M. Edwardes, *Management Today* (March 1983).

7 The results come from a seminar run in 1984 at Brunel University by the authors and D. Guest.

8 F. Shipper and C.S. White, 'Linking organizational effectiveness and environmental change', *Long Range Planning*, vol. 16, no. 3, (1983), pp. 99–106.

9 S. Rothwell, 'Integrating the elements of a company employment policy', *Personnel Management* (November 1984), p. 31.

10 Lord Sieff, 'How I see the personnel function', *Personnel Management* (December 1984), pp. 28–30.

11 J. Hamill, 'Labour relations decision-making within multinational corporations', *Industrial Relations Journal* vol. 15, no. 2 (1984), pp. 30–34.

12 Sir Alex Jarret, Chairman of Reed International at an interview with the authors, 1983.

13 Similar major voluntary redundancy programmes have been completed in other public sector organizations, such as British Shipbuilders and British Steel.

14 D. Plastow, article in *The Guardian*, 11 January 1983.

15 L. Klein, *A Social Scientist in Industry* (London: Gower Press, 1976).

16 P. Hill, *Towards a new philosophy of management* (London: Gower Press, 1971). See also F.H.M. Blacker and C.A. Brown, *Whatever Happened to Shell's New Philosophy of Management?* (Farnborough: Saxon House, 1980).

7
Assessing Efficiency in Personnel Policies

In Chapter 6 we discussed measures of the effectiveness of personnel management. One of the ways in which a personnel department becomes effective is by continuously monitoring the policies for which the department is responsible. We now wish to consider the ways in which the overall efficiency of personnel policies may be monitored. We will begin by reviewing the techniques that are available for auditing specific policies, and for monitoring the personnel function through budgets and reports. We will then go on to examine ways of determining the state of the company's employment relationships as a whole.

Policies are important because of the cost implications and because of the effect they have on the quality, the motivation and the creativity of the people who work for the organization. The precise relationship between the intention of policies, and the actuality of worker performance, is problematic. Not enough is known about the effect of policies on behaviour, and the only way in which one can establish how policies are working is to follow a regular monitoring programme. The case for continuous monitoring is also made by the pace of change, which leads to policy variations to cope with new occupations, new methods and new products. To be functional for the business, the personnel department has to maintain a watching brief on the costs of employment. From this monitoring there is every prospect of new policies emerging. For example, from an appreciation of company car costs, companies have moved to leasing arrangements, or to salary sacrifice schemes which may be a major plan in a flexible benefits policy.

Policies about people must inevitably express values, assumptions and the received wisdom of management about how to motivate, and to create harmonious relationships. Assumptions from the human relations school of thought are present in such areas as job redesign, and joint consultation, and permeate much of organization development theory. Polar opposites are frequently shown in order to represent what seem to be clusters of ideas impressed upon the unconscious mind by repeating patterns of experience as in Blake and Mouton's people versus task orientation,[1] or McGregor's Theory X Theory Y views of people,[2] where we may characterize the environments:

X	Y
Low trust	High trust
Authoritarian style of management	Participation style of management
No risks taken with people	Risk-taking encouraged
Low creativity	High creativity
Boring, repetitive work	Exciting place to work
Inflexible, unresponsive employees	Flexible, motivated workforce

In such a view, management styles which imply high trust and a respect of individuals, where managers listen to their workforce, are contrasted to authoritarian Theory X visions of people, where people are seen as naturally idle and unable to make work decisions for themselves.

Because there are so many situational factors which influence behaviour, it is impossible to demonstrate the 'correctness' of either Theory X or Theory Y. However, among the situational factors that do condition behaviour, personnel policies are significant, not least because they help to create the organization's culture. We have discussed above the way that work people are also seeking to influence their environment, by pushing back the frontiers of control. Frequently, different assumptions are made about working people and managers, supervisors and those performing semi-management tasks. Thus different policies are often applied to managers than those applied to 'shopfloor' employees; for example, on sick pay, holidays, pensions, hours of work, and methods of payment. 'Shopfloor' workers may be required to 'clock on' because their pay is rated by the hour and they may be subject to stricter discipline.

When monitoring personnel policies we are asking two questions:

1 Are the assumptions behind the policy correct? To help answer this question, we need to determine what the assumptions are so we can differentiate between business objectives and social or legal objectives in the policy. Where there are business objectives we can then answer the question by measuring any increments in marginal productivity deriving from the policy.
2 How efficient is the method of conducting the policy? Here we would need to know what are the costs of delivering the policy, compared with any given outcome. This secondary question is concerned with means rather than the desirability of the end, which is resolved by answering question 1.

We face a major difficulty in our monitoring task because we are unable to control those variables that influence behaviour in addition to the policy under scrutiny. Tyson recalls how he conducted a consultancy assignment to harmonize pay and conditions at the British Hydro-mechanics Research Association. BHRA employed 500 people in every imaginable occupational group from cleaners to scientists. As a part of the process a job evaluation scheme was devised to cover all these groups in one reward structure. New promotion, and incremental policies were established. The organization was expanding rapidly in revenue and in personnel, and it is difficult to see how this could have been achieved without harmonization, which brought both flexibility to the organization and a removal of grievances and more cooperation on new work. Policies interrelate, and are also intertwined with the expansion or the contraction of the business, as well as with such influences as the style of the top managers.

In spite of all the difficulties, the need for personnel specialists to ensure that they both help to create wealth and to obtain recognition for their work is such that the attempt to measure performance must be made. As we have outlined, the difficulties of assessment are compounded since the cost structure in most organizations is not designed to reveal the personnel specialists' contribution.

When we survey these contributions, it is useful to distinguish between those that are directly and those that are indirectly attributable to the personnel function. The direct contribution is an estimate of the costs or revenue changes which are immediately expressed in money terms, or which can be quickly translated into amounts of money. The indirect contributions entail a second stage in the process; these are advisory activities not related immediately to output. We have already said how difficult it is to determine the part that specialist personnel staff play in the personnel function which is an aspect of all managerial work.

This is true also of the consultancy service which personnel managers internally offer to their colleague managers. When managers are performing a variety of roles, including those with a specialist personnel aspect, for example a manufacturing manager who determines the need for a manual labour flexibility agreement, disentangling a 'pure' personnel decision for evaluation purposes, is impossible.

Routine monitoring of personnel department activity is evident where there is a 'contracts manager' or 'architect' approach to the personnel job. The more free ranging audit is most likely to be provoked by some outside event: a merger, a new senior management team, threatened industrial action, or in a case known to the authors, when a company's employees were approached by a trade union seeking bargaining rights on their behalf. In so far as we wish to be prescriptive, we would suggest a frequent audit of the overall personnel function of management is in keeping with the notion of human *resource* management, which emphasizes the significance of the people to the business. In the remainder of this chapter we will describe in detail these tactical approaches to the evaluation of personnel policies.

Practical methods of assessment

Three tactical approaches seem feasible. First, an audit of individual policies could be undertaken, in all their aspects to discover the benefits actually achieved from the policy. Second, regular budgetary controls on policies, together with reports on technical efficiency, will give guidance on how efficiently a policy is being conducted. Third, the personnel department could audit the key dimensions in the employment relationship, unconstrained by current policy objectives.

Methods of auditing personnel policies

As managements have become increasingly aware of how high the costs of employment are, one might anticipate a greater interest in the measurement of the personnel function's contribution, and the granting of an improved status to those people who ensure that the money is spent to good purpose. Up until now, the absence of mechanisms for measuring the personnel function's efficiency has inhibited the status of personnel specialists.

For many organizations there seems no reason to separate out employment costs. After all, it could be argued, the time and expense of such an exercise would not be justified by the results. This effect is similar to the assumptions about personnel we described earlier; where senior managers do not believe in personnel techniques they will not monitor the benefits and costs of using them. If selection tests, for instance, are not regarded as valid because personnel selection is believed to rest on the working of arcane, haphazard forces, then there is no point in measuring the costs of a bad decision, since according to this belief, such a decision could not have been avoided.

For some management reporting purposes, the total costs of production or the total costs of sales, including personnel, requires no further breakdown. Accounting conventions also determine how costs are split. Divisions between 'direct' and 'indirect' costs may be convenient for pricing policy or for the allocation of overheads, for example, but are not helpful when assessments of personnel costs are made.

The list of manpower costs is extensive. If we seek to measure the efficiency of personnel management we must consider the question in terms of employment costs. A well-known catalogue of manpower costs was developed by the Manpower Society in 1970.[3] This broke down costs in detail under the headings:

Remuneration

Salary/wages – basic pay, bonus, overtime, shift pay, merit pay, etc.

Direct fringe benefits – car, pension funds, luncheon vouchers, subsidized housing, holidays.

Statutory costs – National Insurance, state pensions, etc.

Recruitment costs
Pre-recruitment – the administration work, preparing job descriptions, person specifications.
Search – advertising, consultancy, 'head hunters'.
Candidate selection – interviewing, testing, medical screening.
Induction – special visits, orientation costs.

Training
Induction training.
Wages while training plus costs of lost production, waste, etc.
Training costs – fees, instructors, training materials, accommodation.
Reports/appraisal – management time, lost production, personnel department costs.

Relocation
Hostel/hotel costs.
Disturbance allowances.
Removal expenses.
Travel expenses.

Leaving costs
Lost production.
Redundancy pay, ex gratia payments, etc.
Retirement costs.

Support costs
Social facilities, subsidies, medical welfare services, safety facilities, security services, insurance premiums.

Manpower administration
Rewards, data processing equipment.
Wage review costs.
'Industrial relations' costs, attendance at JCC, etc.
Manpower research project costs.

   This is a list of historical costs comprising those that are easily identified. The most significant of the costs are the wages, salaries and benefits. However, this list does have limitations. Replacement costs are more important than historical costs, and there is no mention here of the opportunity costs of employing people – when there is a choice, for example, between employment and buying machinery, recruitment or growth through the acquisition of another business. The costs of unsuccessful selection decisions go beyond the money spent on recruitment, training and salaries. One has only to reflect for a moment on the costs of employing an inadequate marketing manager to appreciate what is at stake in recruitment. What is required is a method of measuring the costs of personnel policies, not just parts of personnel systems or the administrative charges incurred.

A study of Allen and Cameron in 1971 showed how manpower costs information was used to audit recruitment, training and reward policies at Bestobell Seals Division.[4] Using the headings developed by the Manpower Society, they show three groups of staff – senior, clerical and semi-skilled operators – employment costs as a percentage of basic salaries (see Table 2).

Table 2   *Employment costs as a percentage of basic pay*

	Other remuneration (O/T shift premia etc.)	Recruitment	Training	Leaving	Support	Administration	Total
Senior staff	25.4	7.0	8.0	5.8	31.4	0.4	78.0
Clerical staff	26.3	2.2	5.8	1.9	10.0	0.5	46.7
Semi-skilled operators	42.6	2.0	3.6	1.9	8.0	0.6	58.7

The high support costs for senior staff reflect the use of the firm's resources for private purposes (whether with authority or not). No relocation costs were included since these were infrequently paid. The computation of these costs and wastage data enabled the company to calculate how a new salary policy for clerical staff which gave more pay increases during the first year of service would reduce costs and be self-financing. A new system of training was introduced aimed at cutting training costs by reducing training time, encouraging labour retention by systematic induction training and increased labour productivity among the 200 operatives by increased labour flexibility. The approach described in this study shows how policies may be amended once sufficient data are available to calculate trade-offs between the various manpower costs. By keeping records under the employment cost headings changes to personnel policies can be monitored under each of the three staff groupings according to the percentage changes to employment costs which occur.

The technique of cost-benefit analysis is a way of trying to make use of information on the costs of policies and the benefits deriving from those policies so that rational decisions can be made, by weighing one against the other. Cost-benefit analysis is a way of ordering priorities, by demonstrating the costs of alternative courses of action, in comparison with the benefits.

The techniques are now well-established, but there are a number of options on which decisions must be made at an early stage. There are so many layers of costs, it is difficult to gauge where to stop. Should opportunity costs be calculated? Would replacement costs provide a more accurate measure than historical costs? In addition to those costs that are obviously attributable to a particular action, there are also 'spill-over' costs which arise from associated actions. For example, if the issue is the costs and benefits resulting from hiving-off a part of the business, should the shut down costs include the possible contribution that the business which is to shut would have made in the future to the remaining business?

When assessing benefits, a decision needs to be made of when the cut-off period should be, over which the stream of benefits is to be evaluated, and the net present value of the benefits or earnings discounted over time. Project appraisal lends itself to cost-benefit analysis, where there are specific pay-off periods by which time the investment is estimated to have been repaid.

There are typical personnel 'projects', such as training and development programmes, which are appropriate for the cost-benefit technique. The costs would include the trainees' wages as well as direct training costs, while the benefits can be found in a steeper learning curve, measured by units of output over time. The technique is less easy to apply to the everyday work of the personnel department, or to the necessarily quick decisions on personnel matters. This is one reason why personnel specialists have used a technique which would help to grant them a more rational way of making decisions only sparingly. Perhaps also the underlying rational ideology of cost-benefit analysis does not accord with the inter-personal pressures and the political alliances of everyday life. In spite of exhortation from academics and the publication of a practical guide aimed at personnel work, by James Cannon[5], it is unusual to find cost-benefit analysis being applied in a pure form to personnel decisions. To be fair, decision-making among most senior managers is usually far removed from the descriptions found in the textbooks of a rational weighing of ends and means. Before we join in the clamour for more systems, or more rational decision-making, let us add two serious reservations about cost-benefit analysis.

1   No complete compendium of costs is possible. The measurement of opportunity costs is necessarily hypothetical. At times of high inflation, replacement costs provide a more accurate basis than historical costs. There is an argument for including only those costs over which management have direct control, although total costs would have to include social as well as business costs, as welfare economists have demonstrated. Finding a layer of costs that is valid for all personnel decisions is extremely difficult, but unless

comparability of costs is achieved, the analysis will be biased, and hence as irrational as any other method. For example, if we take one type of direct cost for the evaluation of recruitment policies, and another type of costs for the evaluation of training policies, it is not possible to make judgements about the relative advantage of, say, recruitment over training when a rapid expansion of senior staff is required.

2 There is often contention about the likely value of any decision within an organization. Different factions may have totally opposing views about a course of action. For example, the marketing department managers may disagree about the value of a new product development. Benefits can suddenly become liabilities, as for example occurred at Rolls-Royce immediately before it collapsed in the 1970s. All the development costs for a new engine became liabilities when a prospective contract was lost. There is frequently no 'objective' benefit for personnel policies; therefore there is not only the question of who benefits, but also the question of who says who benefits.

There are thus a number of caveats we would extend to the use of cost-benefit analysis in making day-to-day personnel decisions. At the micro level, decision-making is too complex, and the 'political' groupings are too significant for any technique that ignores the pragmatism of the moment. It remains a useful general approach, however. Even if the final decision is affected by value judgements, it is helpful for the personnel specialist to have established in monetary terms the costs and benefits of policies.

Where it is not possible to provide a reliable assessment of the benefits, a cost minimization method could be adopted. This would result in seeking the least costly solution to a problem, for a given amount of output or activity. This is best used where no direct return on the investment is sought. Let us take two instances. One application for such an approach would be when making judgements about management development, where benefits are difficult to assess. A cost minimization approach would help the manager to choose between different alternatives, provided the extent of the management development activities was similar. The problem arises where a decision has to be made comparing two different courses of action, without knowing the benefits of each.

As another example, a cost minimization approach could be helpful when deciding how to deal with public relations. No accurate measure of return on the expenditure is likely, and given that one could spend unlimited sums on PR activities, a level has to be set which is commensurate with the image the organization wishes to portray. One could then seek to minimize costs to a point where any further reductions would make an incontrovertible difference to the projection of the image.

Until recently, there were practical objections to cost-benefit analysis. The data were inaccessible, or the price for extracting it was exorbitant. The information revolution has now broken down the most serious practical objections to the technique.

Investments in new personnel policies should bring improvements in company performance. This still leaves the question of whether personnel policies are typically aimed at long-run performance, or at the resolution of immediate problems. As we argued in Chapter 3, we would anticipate that company survival in both the short and long term would be a necessary pre-condition of any policy, so even if a policy is intended to make a long-term contribution, it would still have to ensure short-term survival.

When measuring productivity improvement, inter-plant or inter-branch comparisons are often made. For example, the Ford Motor Company in the UK is often compared with Ford in Germany. Similarly, research has been conducted and comparisons are often researched at national level.[6] However, broad international comparisons are not useful in isolating those personnel policies which can improve productivity, because there are so many cultural, social and economic variables, such as hours of work, government subsidies, employee consumption and expenditure patterns which conceal changes at the company level of analysis.

It is precisely because there are so many variables over which managers do not have control that personnel policies are so important. Here at least there are strategies and programmes which managers can direct.

One of the chief hindrances to the manipulation of policy is failure to find satisfactory measures of the results. An approach which has tempted personnel specialists and academics alike as offering a measure of the value of people to the organization is called 'Human Resource Accounting', or 'Human Asset Accounting'. Flamholtz and Lacey defined this approach in the following way:

> Human resource accounting may be defined as the measurement and
> reporting of the cost and value of people as organizational resources. It
> involves accounting for investment in people and their replacement costs, as
> well as accounting for the economic values of people to an organization.[7]

They go on to describe the value of an employee to the firm as 'the present value of the difference between wage and marginal revenue product. An employee's value derives from the ability of the firm to pay less than the marginal revenue product.'

The general argument is that there are distinct investments in the employees, through education of a generalized kind undertaken by society, and specific job or career-related training, funded in part by the company and by the employee (in reduced earnings), which together with the costs of employment, represent investments in people which should be measurable.

There seem to be a diversity of ways of measuring the investments. Most typically, the historic ('acquisition' cost) or the replacement cost is taken, and the human asset balance is depreciated annually, according to the employee's expected working life. Normally, only those costs that derive from the employment are measured; earlier (and not insignificant) costs incurred by society are ignored. In other schemes, the 'human capital value' represented by the total payroll can be taken, and a further refinement is to discount these earnings over time. More complex methods have been proposed using psychological measures of satisfaction, and of effort, to arrive at a value to the organization. Further variants on these include multiplying performance ratings by wage costs, and there are individual measures of value based on expected earnings over a period of time.

The major benefit to be derived from human resource accounting is that employees are perceived as assets, not just as costs. The notion of 'investing' in employees encourages a view that one is looking for the profit to be gained from the investment and therefore the focus is on the development of people for a purpose. In addition to this positive slant, human resource accounting practices may help managers to improve the accuracy of their decisions, for example when calculating the cost of redundancy.

Unfortunately, most of the attempts to measure people as financial assets have failed. There is often confusion with the terms because of accounting conventions, and there are theoretical weaknesses in each of the three main measures used: capitalized human resource investments, human capital value, and net present value to the firm. Further, human assets are perceived to be changeable. There are some individuals whom one would regard as liabilities rather than assets, although they may be retained; for example because it is hoped they will improve or because they have served the employer well in the past. Indeed, there may be no agreement among management on whether individual employees are assets or liabilities. These 'assets' are outside the direct control of management, which can have no owners' rights over them, and only in large monopolistic firms can management influence the labour market. At its worst, human asset accounting is just another way of describing costs; at its best it is a step towards an overall measure of efficiency of personnel policies.

The utility of human asset accounting is demonstrated by a study of industrial engineers in the US Navy, undertaken by Flamholtz and Geis.[8] A 'human resource replacement cost' model was developed after an analysis of the recruitment, selection and training costs incurred in a single tier recruitment structure, where a 'position replacement cost' was established for each level of industrial engineer. A number of career paths were used for engineers to rise to supervisry positions. The costs were split between acquisition costs (including recruitment and promotion costs) and total development costs (including orientation costs, formal training costs, informal on-the-job training costs, etc.). By comparing the costs of different career paths, it was possible to show which strategy for human resources development was most cost-effective.

Other applications for their model are claimed by the authors who see the possible use of replacement cost information in such areas as the allocation or utilization of people, costs of labour turnover and compensation. Like cost-benefit analysis, human asset accounting seems a useful general approach which provides opportunities for auditing personnel policies.

Budgetary controls and reports on technical efficiency

A recognition of personnel costs is useful both for long-term planning and for short-term control. The interaction between the short and the long term is infrequently acknowledged. Strategic decisions are often taken with an eye to the long term, but without recognition of the effect on immediate costs. In corporate planning, global figures are sometimes quoted without a sufficient analysis, making it impossible for the human resource aspects of the plan to be monitored. In our description of the 'contracts manager' personnel model, we discussed this model's emphasis on 'systems'. The costs of these systems might be measured, but it requires a broader vision of the personnel function to combine measures of costs with the notion of effectiveness. Thus, the question, 'how much does running our appraisal system cost?', might be asked, but the prior question, 'why do we have appraisal schemes and how do they contribute to the success of the business?', is asked only where the broader vision of personnel management as integral to the business plan is possessed.

A good example is the personnel department performance indicators used by Granada TV Rental.[9] Ratios such as

$$\frac{\text{Actual training costs} \times 100}{\text{Training budget}}$$

and

$$\frac{\text{Training budget}}{\text{Average staff budgeted for}} \text{ £ per head}$$

may be valuable if there are several similar personnel departments within the same group, where comparisons may be made. However, without a wider statement of purpose related to that year's business objectives, this type of ratio reveals only the technical efficiency of the department. It is still significant, and a sign of the times, that Granada TV Rental's personnel function has sought to install a quantitative measurement system, and to produce an annual report for the Board, showing what has been achieved.

There are a number of measures that attempt to show the cost-effectiveness of the personnel function. Many organizations now use company performance indicators in comparison with the number of employees. These indicators include:

Sales value per employee
Sales volume per employee
Profit per employee
Added value per employee
Capital per employee
Costs per employee

Employment costs are often shown as ratios. For example employee costs as a percentage of:

Sales value
Sales volume
Profit
Added value
Cash flow

The main benefit of using ratios such as these derives from relating employment costs to productivity. As we have already commented, company performance is influenced by many factors, and we must therefore look for the particular ways in which personnel policies may affect these ratios. Policies on manning levels, deployment, reward structures, training, organization structure, communication and employee involvement can all contribute. What is required, therefore, is that the objectives of these policies be expressed in terms of the ratios described above. For example, redeployment and selective redundancy might improve the ratio of employee costs to sales value, and reward policies could be designed to improve the ratio of employee costs to added value. The efficiency of reward policies may also be measured by comparing changes to output, with changes in pay.[10] Similarly, the influence of incentive schemes may be measured by examining the difference in output for any given level of incentive payment. To measure the efficiency with which salaries are administered, the 'compa ratio' may be adopted, which shows what is actually happening to the salaries of a group of people in a grade or salary band.

In the field of rewards policy, we thus have three measures,

1 A measure of efficiency of the overall policy and its contribution to effectiveness:

$$\frac{\text{Sales}}{\text{Total compensation for employees}} \text{ for each unit}$$

2 A measure of a sales incentive scheme, or new reward policy

    Compare % incentive change:% volume change

3 A measure of the efficiency of the salary administration

    Compa ratio:

$$\text{By grade } \frac{\text{Average salary}}{\text{Midpoint of range}} \times 100$$

Variances between policy objectives at these three levels and achievements will occur, but at least with performance indicators we may discover the reason. For example, compa ratios often go below 100 when there has been attrition of salaries in that grade, because of large numbers of new starts, which typically enter the scale below the midpoint.

Information technology in the personnel function

The information revolution has arrived at personnel's door. For a number of years, personnel functions have been busy advising others on the effects of new technology: new technology agreements, altered work practices, and new work design. In the last five years, new information technologies have been brought into the operation of personnel activities, with the objective of improving personnel decisions.

There are various areas of personnel management which are information-intensive – only one aspect has a history of automated processing: payroll. Recruitment, manpower planning, management development, employee relations negotiating, computer-based training, absence management and, of course, the ubiquitous 'administration' are now prime targets for computerization.

There is no doubt that a prime motive among personnel professionals for introducing some type of electronic data processing has been to improve their performance. Electronic data processing (whether a 'computer' of some scale or sophisticated word processor installations) is seen as an effective way of reducing the present range of personnel management commitments more efficiently or, at a minimum, with the same level of resources. The latter point has in recent years been of significant importance. Personnel departments have not been immune from headcount reductions, have not escaped the attention of work study departments charged with seeking out labour intensive operations and recommending the application of the scalpel.

Increased efficiency is apparent in many personnel management departments through electronic data processing. No personnel department of any significant size would today be running its recruitment management without word processing technology, for example. But there is an inherent danger in thinking exclusively in these terms. Electronic data processing in personnel management can do more than achieve efficiency improvements in existing activities, if personnel practitioners are alive to the opportunities and seize them.

The most frequent justification for new technology investment is cost substitution, since it is possible to undertake more work with only the cost of the machinery and its maintenance to bear. However, new technology can be used to improve management decision-making by producing reports which were not possible before, granting opportunities to senior management for improving the business by cutting out inefficient parts and extending profitable activities.

In short, there is the opportunity not merely to 'computerize' what is now done in the hope that it will bring efficiency improvements to existing workloads, but also to extend the use of manpower information into management decision-taking, to move personnel further along the route of total integration with business decision-taking.

This latter process might be called the 'think again' movement. The question is not what we do and how can electronic data processing help us do it more speedily, efficienctly and with less staff; but what do we want? What kind of manpower information in terms of its nature, scope and detail do we want to hold?

Applying our models to this argument, we could say that our 'clerk of works' approach would strive for efficiency, would be proud of the increased accuracy and the enhanced range of reports electronic data processing could bring about. Our 'contracts manager' model department will recognize the opportunity to introduce new data, more penetrating in what it tells the reader about the employee population and more related to decision-taking. The 'architect' model department will start from the position that information of the highest grade is the basic building block of strategic human resources management. The computer will not be placed on a pedestal, but will be the everyday workhorse, the manpower information data base, the central nervous system through which all personnel management decisions are analysed into their various component parts.

This approach is exemplified by the simple but effective use of computerized records of absence at May and Baker, where the capacity to process masses of data and feed it back to the responsible line managers, showing comparative absence rates between departments reduced absenteeism and resulted in major cost savings for the company.[11]

Reports using labour turnover and stability are often used to judge the impact of policies on morale and the quality of relationships. Among the quantitative measures used, probably the most popular are indices of labour stability, and labour turnover. These are normally determined in the following way:

Annual labour turnover:

Central or ('BIM') rate $= \dfrac{\text{No. of leavers at end of year}}{\substack{\text{Average number employed} \\ \text{during the year}}} \times 100$

Stability Index $= \dfrac{\substack{\text{No. with more than one} \\ \text{year's service}}}{\text{Total employed one year ago}} \times 100$

Stability and turnover may be taken together to discover whether or not there is a widespread turnover problem, or if it is confined to a few jobs, turning over frequently.

Labour turnover	Stability	
High	Low	Widespread turnover problem
High	High	Fringe turnover problem Stable core of jobs
Low	High	Very stable labour situation

The calculation of labour turnover is essential for any manpower planning process. But, as an index, it is frequently used to assess the value of personnel policies, or as a diagnostic tool, to establish where the problems are.

One of the immediate difficulties encountered is to find an answer to the question, what should the rate of labour turnover be? Without a 'norm', there is little one can do with labour turnover data as an assessment of the personnel function. There has been much research into wastage, and we know that wastage rates are usually specific to length of service, to age and to geographical area. They also vary according to occupational groups, and there are variations over time, as external factors influence job-change decisions, for example seasonality effects and the effects of unemployment. Given these factors, establishing what the 'norm' is now for, say, senior secretaries in central London, is problematic. With some occupations, there are imprecise definitions; for example, there are many different types of accounts clerks, salesmen and personnel managers!

One of the more useful techniques for judging the causes of labour turnover is therefore to compare the group in question against a control group in the same organization, if this is possible. Similarly, a cohort analysis can be undertaken of an occupational group and the variations to its characteristics as a population can be studied and associated with any changes that have taken place in personnel policy, such as a new rewards structure. However, once again we must be wary of assuming that an association is necessarily a casual relationship. There may be a third, as yet unidentified, variable, which is influencing the two variables we are studying.

There are other quantitative measures which help to give a picture of the 'stability' of an organization, if combined with stability, turnover indices and qualitative data. Here, the most obvious measures would be of days lost through disputes, accidents, absenteeism and sickness. There are few complications in gathering these statistics; again, the major problems derive from how to interpret them.

The number of days lost through 'industrial disputes' would certainly be one way of determining the efficacy of the employee relations policy in a company, but low productivity and bad industrial relations are not necessarily related. In one study, output from coal mines which had a large number of days lost through disputes compared favourably with mines where the number of days lost due to industrial action was low.[12] Apathy, poor workmanship, slow production methods are not reflected in the strike record. Strikes might be encouraged by the management, as part of a long-term strategy; for example, to reduce the inventory, or to weaken the union prior to a major challenge.

Qualitative judgements are more likely to be of value here. For example, an audit of the grievance procedures, which examine the kind of issues raised and how they were dealt with gives much more direct evidence of the quality of relationships.

Accident statistics are often thought to reveal information about training, interest in the work, and morale, as well as data on the organization's accident prevention policies. Absenteeism and sickness absence may also be used as thermometers to measure the general health of the organization as an employer. Statistics on the average days lost by age groups, length of service and status or occupational group, could be used to estimate the utility of employment decisions on hours of work, shift patterns, transport facilities and relocation, as well as specific programmes such as the medical screening of new employees, welfare, health improvement schemes such as influenza vaccination and, of course, the effect of the sick pay arrangements themselves. In a more general sense, policies aimed at promoting the well-being of the employees may also be judged inferentially from these statistics. Job satisfaction schemes, flexible working hours arrangements and working conditions may be thought to have an influence on absence statistics. To use statistics in this way would require a test, with all the rigour of any statistical test: care in the sampling procedures, tests before and after the introduction of the new policy and control of any other variables that might influence the sample population.

Auditing the employment relationship
A 'total' approach which seeks to audit the overall personnel function of management requires firstly the identification of those dimensions of the employment relationship that influence company performance. The contribution of the specialist personnel department is to advise, correct, audit and where required to control these key areas. The benefit of such an approach is that it looks seriously at the interaction of personnel policies. Some of the data required for an overall audit would be generated by the

regular monitoring procedures we have just described, but in some cases a special investigation is necessary.

To demonstrate this approach, we have shown a typical list of key areas, with an indication of the data sources we would use to find the answer to the questions posed.

Reward structures

What behaviour do we seek to encourage, and how successful is our present pay policy in achieving this?

Methods

Examine added value per employee, make comparisons where possible.
Compare output data between departments, and ratio of wages: output.
Review variable payment schemes, determine reasons why some employees actually achieve better results than others.
Compare appraisal data with salary review recommendations.
Compare achievements in rewards with policy objectives.
Examine costs of employment by occupational group.
Examine overtime payments by department.

Communications

What do people in different parts of the organization know about our objectives, and what do they care about them?

Methods

Conduct a communication audit using an outside consultant. (This might entail a questionnaire for staff and 'workshop' type seminars.)
Audit current communication channels. Look at information passed up and down, and how this is done.
Use current channels to monitor briefing groups, Joint Consultative Committees.

Worker/management relationships

How productive are the relationships between supervisors and those being managed?

Methods

Audit disputes procedures – how many disagreements, how long before resolved?
Audit grievance procedures – how many, how long to solve?
Audit discipline procedures – how many cases, with what results?
Departmental analysis of absenteeism, and of accidents.
Employee morale survey.
Labour turnover/stability data.
Examine functioning of joint consultative machinery.
Output levels by department.
Time lost through disputes.
Frequency of change in supervision.

Training of supervisors.
Perceived authority of supervision.

Employee quality
How relevant are the skills of our employees, and do we have enough of what we need?

Methods
Prepare skills inventory.
Produce headcount × skill × service in post.
Assessment centre data on managers.
Appraisal reports – analysis of high potential employees, study reports, actual performance and individual histories (promotions, salary increases).
Customer complaints, analysed by department.
Measures of output per employee.
Manpower forecasts of skills needed.
Management development strategies.

These lists are intended to illustrate the key areas and the techniques for examining them. No doubt readers will be able to add to the lists according to the needs of their own organization. An audit of this kind need not be a static piece of research. The very act of auditing the relationship can be used to enhance the relationship by involving employees in giving feedback on a regular basis about their views.

Perhaps the best way of discovering information about the quality of the employment relationship is to ask the questions directly, through attitude surveys. These require some sophistication and care in design. They are, however, becoming increasingly popular as part of an overall strategy to improve employee relations, especially as a device for opening up new channels of communication with employees. By establishing a channel parallel to the trade unions, employers can still bargain through the union but are able simultaneously to develop direct links with their workers, thus gaining quicker feedback on policy initiatives and a chance to gain the commitment of employees through a measure of participation.

Attitude surveys can be used to measure a variety of employee reactions. There are a number of techniques, the best known method being a questionnaire tailored to the requirements of the company. These large-scale surveys have the benefit of gathering data from the whole company. As part of the evaluation of a programme, there is much to be said for this type of direct feedback. A typical example of this approach was the instrument developed to measure the quality of work life at General Motors. This was a product of the company's organization development department. Its head, Howard Carlson, wrote:

> The original interest came out of GM's measurement philosophy. The notion of evaluating what you're doing is basic in General Motors. Also, as a

behavioural scientist, I have to say learn as we go. So we lay research on what we do. When we do research, we do it in a way that always involves the line organization rather than sitting next to the computer and playing little games with it.[13]

Significantly, the evaluation of their programme was used to help gain acceptance for organization development intentions in GM. There are other methods of gaining direct feedback from employees. For example, at a large printing company, the Chairman organized a 'phone-in' from his employees, so that direct communication with the staff was encouraged on any subject they thought was of concern.

To summarize, what seems to be required to gain an impression of employee satisfaction in terms of morale, stability and employment relationships, is a variety of measures. Quantitative measures give a picture of aggregates of people which need support with direct evidence, in the form of reports and impressions from management. Any measure needs a weighting to attach importance. Here again, the numbers and the strength of the feeling are what counts, and both qualitative and quantitative measures are required for this.

Personnel policies are designed to assist in the management of transitions for individuals, as well as to help maintain the organization's stability. These transitions include the selection, induction, training, promotion, transfer, demotion, dismissal, retirement and redundancy activities in which changes for individuals are managed by the personnel function. An important area of evaluation is therefore the ease with which these transitions are arranged and carried through.

What is being judged is the personnel manager's role in both the development of policies to meet these contingencies, and the way the policies are conducted. In most instances the personnel manager's role will be intertwined with the roles of line managers. Again, this draws our attention to the effectiveness of the personnel manager as a 'consultant'. For example, the establishment of relationships, the use of influencing skills and the quality of the advice given will be decisive in the success of the transitions.

A simple example here would be the support and coaching required at the time of a promotion. The effectiveness of the personnel function in this instance would be judged on two levels. First, the achievements of the 'development' system (appraisal, identification of potential, developmental activities) in producing a successor at the right time, and second, the way the promotion itself is dealt with. The development policy could be said to be effective if as a result, the capacities, needs and aspirations of individuals are in accord with the opportunities available, within a time frame which suited the changes in the organization. But the effectiveness of the personnel function would also be judged by the actions agreed between the manager and the personnel manager aimed at overcoming any perceived weaknesses of the person newly promoted, and which provide support and coaching. The support from colleagues and new subordinates may also be conditional upon their view of the fairness of the selection, which implies that the method of selecting people for promotion is also important for achieving a successful transition.

The evaluation of the performance of the personnel function in relation to individuals is likely to be based largely on the outcomes of its policies, and thus on the performance of the people recruited, promoted, transferred, etc. This evaluation is by those within the same employment network and by customers who make judgements about the quality of the service they are receiving, which may be manifested by complaints or by increased orders.

In addition to qualitative judgements about individuals, line managers are also watchful of the lead times associated with transitions. How long they think it should take to recruit say a systems analyst, an electronic engineer or a finance manager will depend on their experience and understanding of the current labour markets for these occupations. The evaluation could again be said to be of the way the personnel manager has acted as a consultant. In this instance, the personnel manager is responsible for creating, or modifying, the line manager's expectations of what an acceptable lead time should be.

All judgements about the effectiveness of the personnel function in managing transitions are influenced by the inevitable use of subjective criteria. One of the most problematic of these is in the evaluation of effective performance. For non-managerial work, this seems usually to be defined by the pace and results of other experienced workers, or as a consequence of rate-fixing where payment by results schemes are used.

The length of time that elapses before the new employee reaches an acceptable standard gives a broad measure of the effectiveness of induction and training schemes. However, given all the intervening variables, such as changes in technology, the management style of supervisors, the manipulation of rates by workers, foremen and union representatives, and the effect of peer group relationships, this can only be a crude measure of training effectiveness.

Probationary and appraisal reports are also a means of evaluating the effectiveness of selection, induction and training. We should remind ourselves of the biases built into such reports. The conjunction between line and personnel managers may multiply the biases rather than reduce them, and at least will render the cause of success or failure difficult to prove. Is the training so good that even a poor recruit has been made successful, or has a good recruit been mismanaged, and despite his aptitude, become disillusioned, and demotivated? These are questions which might be asked, for example.

There are quantitative techniques, which may be used to infer the success or failure of policies. We mentioned in the previous section, the use of labour turnover indices, accident rates and so on. To these may be added faults analysis, and measures of the scrap produced, as well as the measurement of output on what is usually called the learning curve. There will already be measures of effective performance in most organizations, and hence it would be sensible to utilize these as a guide to the capacity of personnel policies to cope successfully with transitions.

One of the difficulties we must face in discussing the measurement of the effectiveness of personnel policies is the absence in many instances of clear objectives. As we outlined in Chapter 3, there may be an overall philosophy of management and for example, there is often a tacit objective in transfer or redundancy policies that the individual will go through the transition feeling that the company has acted fairly and that compensation for the disruption caused is at least adequate. In the whole area of welfare policies, objectives are diffuse, and can only be summarized as being aimed at granting the individual a sufficient sense of well-being to prevent disruption to the work. Other than attitude surveys, critical incident evaluation and the normal reports from managers, and joint consultative committees, there are no special techniques for evaluating the effectiveness of these policies. For line managers, this work is largely an exercise in getting rid of people problems. For senior managers it is not only the problems, which may result from a number of factors, but also the ease with which problems have been identified which will assist in their evaluation of personnel management.

One reason why no such techniques have emerged is because the policies are diffuse in their objectives, and the responsibilities for conducting the policies are widespread. Usually, no one group of people is charged with the development and execution of this range of work. Where specialists in particular policies have emerged, so the evaluation of their contribution is encouraged.

A good example of this is in the whole field of training and development. Up to the 1960s, there were few training specialists operating at a high level in companies. Training instructors were largely within the control of line managers, conducting job-related training. With a recognition of the need for policies accented towards the development of managers, specialist roles have been created, and hence the felt need for evaluation has started. Paradoxically, as the policy-makers set the objectives, they tend to use their own frameworks, which are often so broad that measurement of achievement is impossible. This is especially true with the open-ended activities to which companies become committed when objectives are set in terms of the development of the individual.

Although evaluation of the training objectives themselves is often not done, in relation to any overall goals, such as profit, the evaluation of learning is intrinsic to the process by which people learn. Evaluation by trainers, and by trainees themselves, is common therefore. A variety of techniques, such as repertory grid administered before and after the training, questionnaires, observation of behaviour, tests and written reports of projects, are used. Managers frequently use appraisal documents as a source of data both on training needs and in subsequent periods, on how these needs have been met. Trainers can break down the process into the evaluation of the design, the content and the methods of training.

A useful typology for examining evaluation has been developed by Hesseling, and is reproduced in Table 3.[14] This demonstrates that the method of assessment varies according to the person who is making it, and for whom the assessment is made. The problem is that evaluation is not systematic, or comprehensive. As Hesseling comments: 'Policy-makers rely usually on the judgement of training supervisors if other evidence is lacking.'[15]

Summary

In this chapter we have been concerned with ways of monitoring personnel policies in terms of their efficiency. We have discussed three approaches: the auditing of individual policies, budgetary controls and reports, which are now facilitated by electronic data processing, and a broader audit of the key dimensions in the employment relationship.

It is possible to produce data which can improve personnel decision-making. Monitoring personnel policies is a fruitful way of both demonstrating the value of the personnel role, and of ensuring the functionality of the policies themselves. There are many practical ways in which personnel managers contribute to productivity. The assessment of the personnel department from different perspectives will inevitably result in different kinds of evaluation, and this reinforces the need to see personnel policies as integrated parts of a coherent plan which can be audited through those dimensions which influence employee performance.

Notes

1 R.R. Blake and J.S. Mouton, *The Managerial Grid* (Gulf, 1964).
2 D. McGregor, *The Human Side of Enterprise* (New York: McGraw-Hill, 1960).
3 Manpower Society, Report of the Manpower Costs Working Party.
   D. York, and C. Dooley, Checking the manpower costs, *Personnel Management* (June 1970).
4 K.R. Allen and K.G. Cameron, 'Manpower costing in action', *Personnel Management* (February 1971).
5 J. Cannon, *Cost Effective Personnel Decisions* (London: IPM, 1979).
   B. Thomas, J. Moxham and J.A.G. Jones, 'A cost-benefit analysis of industrial training', *British Journal of Industrial Relations* vol. VII, no. 2 (1969).
6 See, for example, the research funded by the Anglo-German Foundation for the Study of Industrial Society, and articles such as P. Finlay, 'Overmanning: Germany v Britain', *Management Today* (August 1981).
7 E.G. Flamholtz and J.M. Lacey, *Personnel Management: human capital theory and human resource accounting* (University of California, Los Angeles: Institute of Industrial Relations, 1981), p. 57.

Table 3 *Typology of evaluations*

Assessment by whom	Assessment for whom				
	Trainees	Trainers	Supervisors	Policy-makers	Scientists
Trainees	1 gradual clarification of learning process; looking glass for each other's behaviour	2 feedback from learner-teacher relation; process control	3 reporting personal impressions	4 reporting personal impressions (usually via superiors)	5 data for further analysis; direct observation, interviews, tests
Trainers	6 feedback from teacher–learner relation; steering evaluation	7 exchange of experiences, e.g. trainers' conferences	8 formal reporting on activities	9 reporting suggestions for follow-up (usually via supervisors)	10 data for further analysis; first step evaluation
Supervisors	11 formal appraisal based upon job performance and training appraisal	12 depending on position of trainer; appraisal or indication for support	13 exchange of experience; preparation for policy	14 major indication for success or failure, suggestions for policy	15 data for further analysis; organizational variables
Policy makers	16 sometimes formal introduction or conclusion of training programme	17 depending on position; determination of training objectives and general standards of performance	18 formal appraisal of training activities	19 general appraisal of training objectives and means; long-term policy	20 organizational variables and starting point for evaluation research
Scientists	21 in adapted form material for reading and lecturing	22 guidelines for improved training; standards of training	23 support for appraisal; standards of performance	24 preparation for decision-making; practical prognoses	25 understanding dynamics of change; methodology and theory of change

8 E.G. Flamholtz and G. Geis, 'The development and implementation of a replacement cost model for measuring human capital: a field study', *Personnel Review*, vol. 13, no. 2 (1984).

9 A. Fowler, 'Proving the personnel department earns its salt', *Personnel Management* (May 1983).

10 J.R. Lapointe, 'Human resource performance indexes', *Personnel Journal* (July 1983).

11 A. Fell, 'Putting a price on lost time', *Personnel Management* (April 1983).

12 W.H. Scott *et al.*, *Coal and Conflict* (Liverpool: Liverpool University Press, 1963).

13 H. Carlson, 'GM's quality of work life efforts', *Personnel* (August 1978).

14 P. Hesseling, *Strategy of Evaluation Research*, (Van Gorcum and Company, 1966), p. 67.

15 ibid., p. 62.

8
Managing Human Resources into the Next Decade

Fortune telling is now a respectable activity. 'Futurology' – the study of trends and speculation on what the future might bring – is an attractive pastime. Predictions range from those which give an Orwellian picture of how future societies may exist, to the more prosaic forecasts emanating from Government and the business schools.

A rash of books on the future, envisaging a major change in our life style has informed the discussion of what might be coming.[1] There are two opposite positions on what may happen. On the one hand, there are those who argue that the possibility of ever improving living standards is enhanced by the new technology. The redefinition of work and leisure has consequences for families, careers and for individual freedoms. In this scenario, the only question that remains to be answered is how to organize our affairs to ensure an equitable distribution of wealth.

Against this view is the notion that a more fundamental genus of alienation is in prospect. Large-scale unemployment could create a permanent class of poor people, with no hope except revolution. The developments in new technology could be used to undermine privacy, trust and relationships, and to control the daily existence of the ordinary people, as Orwell's version of 1984 foretold. The new technologies, structural unemployment, the growth of newly industrialized countries, and political realignments are harbingers of widescale social change.

The world recession, which has had such a dramatic influence on the United Kingdom, and on other industrialized nations has coincided with the introduction of new technologies to both the manufacturing and service sectors of the economy, and with a reawakening among new developed nations of an economic nationalism on which their survival depends. We will complete our evaluation of the personnel function of management by considering the impact of change on personnel work, and the prospects for new models emerging in the future.

When we contemplate the range of variables which are likely to have a major effect on the personnel role as the twentieth century comes to a close, the most striking features are the amount of change, the pace of change, and the way people naturally adjust to new ways of thinking and working. From a content analysis of newspapers in the USA, Naisbitt described a series of 'megatrends' which he claimed were clues to the direction our lives are taking.[2] In addition to following the idea that we are moving from an 'industrial' to an 'information society', he argues that people are recognizing the increasing importance of human, social and spiritual values in response to the potentially alienating effects of new advanced technology. With better communications comes an awareness of the impact of world economic trends upon local societies, and thus we see a shift from short-term to long-term thinking and planning, and from centralization to decentralization. Consistent with this theme are the trends towards self-help, to participating democracy, to networks and away from hierarchies, and towards multiple options rather than either/or choices.

In practice, changes may be said to take place at different levels. At a societal level, that is what we experience as outside ourselves, as part of 'society' there are a number of fundamental influences on personnel policies which we have stressed throughout this book. We can briefly summarize these as follows:

Unemployment

High levels of unemployment, caused by increases in the labour supply, and by the dual effects of new technology and the recession, seem inevitable in the medium term. Although there are still skill shortages, those most at risk of unemployment are the poorly qualified, and those whose skills have become obsolete.[3]

Government policy
Most governments in Europe have responded pragmatically to the challenge of change, without any coordinated policy on unemployment from the EEC.[4] In France, for example, the Government has passed three decrees designed to promote part-time working, to reform fixed-term contracts and to give greater flexibility in employment in order to help the long-term unemployed.[5] The approach adopted by the British Government has been to concentrate on a supply side policy. The theory is that by improving the basic core skills used in most jobs, and by developing aptitudes among young people, by 'freeing' the labour market from legal and trade union restrictions, the price mechanism will allocate labour at pay rates which help new business to develop, and initially through exports, the economy will start to recover. The expanded Youth Training Scheme, the 'Open Tech', the Graduate Enterprise Programme, the reduced role of wages councils, less protection against unfair dismissal and legislation aimed at limiting trade union power are therefore consistent aspects of a central theme.[6]

New technology and occupational structure

The recession and the consequential structural unemployment have masked the impact of new technology on the number of jobs, but its influence on the type of work undertaken is more clearly seen. We are witnessing a shift from blue-collar to white-coat jobs in manufacturing, where computer-aided design and computer-aided manufacturing systems are now much more common. The accent in manufacturing has shifted towards high quality with as small a labour component as possible, and with quality, output, workflow and costs monitored by electronic means.[7] In the service sector, automatic tellers in banks, cashless transactions, word processing and electronic mail can now readily be found. However, the basic problems of supervision remain. Recruitment, motivation, reward, training, development, and discipline are just as difficult. In many companies the push towards a more economic use of resources has resulted in tiers of management being cut from the hierarchy, and to a greater reliance on the first-line supervisor, who now has electronic processing of data as an aid to control.

Changes in the structure of jobs

A number of authors have pointed to the new approaches to work which new technology and unemployment will bring. The analysis by Handy suggests a redefinition of work as a necessary prerequisite to the solution of the unemployment problem.[8] His optimistic scenario envisages that a broader definition of work will emerge to include the black economy, and all the voluntary activities people perform, for which payment will be made; the working life will thus be halved. With new technology providing the wealth, organizations could become federations, with individuals working from what Toffler called the 'electronic cottage'.[9]

The value of Handy's study lies in his ventilation of the unemployment problem, and his interesting speculations about its solution. However, economic problems would seem to inhibit the emergence of the more optimistic scenario, especially the difficulties of redistributing wealth. History indicates that those who acquire wealth will go to extraordinary lengths to retain it, as the history of many old English families reveals. British commerce and industry is highly concentrated into the hands of a few, and there is no practical means of achieving a revolutionary change without a political revolution.

A variety of organizational forms seem possible, and a diversity of psychological contracts between workers and management are likely. We might expect a polarization between soft contracting, with sophisticated management of the internal labour market, and hard contracting, where organizations become the hub of a range of bought-in services, franchises, consultancy and sub-contract arrangements, where employees are treated as a flexible resource, with what may be described as an organic approach to organization structure.[10]

The business environment

Areas of growth in the British economy have been innovative companies, which have concentrated in new specialized fields. If we measure performance in terms of net profit as a percentage of invested capital, there were many giant companies performing badly in 1983 and 1984.[11] One might anticipate more takeovers of the unprofitable companies, to create bigger units with the intention of making better use of the capital employed. Competitiveness might also be improved by divestment, and more joint ventures. However, in the longer term it is the development of new products rather than slow incremental change to existing ranges which will pull the highly industrialized economies out of recession, as the 1980s draw to a close. This implies more research and development activity, and better product design, as well as the coordination of marketing, selling and engineering or technical functions to mount major drives in the sale of high quality products. Success depends on the effective management of the change process itself, by personnel and top management teams. Multi-disciplinary project teams also require adjustments to management style, good communications and careful selection.

Employment costs

There is a European-wide movement by trade unions to reduce hours of work, and to increase holidays. In the UK this has happened across a wide range of occupations. The trend towards an increased entitlement to holidays with pay has reached the stage where by the end of 1984, 95% of manual workers subject to national collective agreements had a minimum of four weeks, and nearly 20% had a minimum entitlement of five weeks.[12] The increased use of part-time workers has in part offset this trend, but the costs of employing people seem to rise inexorably. Government regulations, such as those over sick pay, have tended to shift the administration costs back onto the employer.

As companies now start to turn the corner of the recession, they are poised either to repeat the mistakes of the past, to accede to high wage claims, to allow overmanning, to underinvest, or to use new technology and better management skills and techniques in order to maintain the high levels of productivity achieved during the recession. As the demand for goods and services increases, the evidence so far is that organizations wish to sustain the greater levels of efficiency obtained at such a high cost. However, the real pressure of increased demand has not yet been felt. The jobs which are being lost are often at the low-paid end, and as blue-collar jobs change to become 'white-coat' jobs for technologists, there is a drift upwards in pay rates. Although earnings have suffered with the recession, basic rates have not, and an upturn in demand may lead to high overtime earnings, and other premia, as companies attempt to cope with extra work without extra employment as well as the pressure for shorter hours.

As the costs of employment have risen more than the earnings of employees in the last few years, we may anticipate that there will be pressure on employers to avoid a conventional expansion of the workforce in line with demand.[13] Instead, we would expect the new forms of more flexible employment contracts to develop, with more self-employment and the loan of venture capital to employees, to enable them to establish complementary businesses. Personnel specialists will therefore need to be flexible and imaginative as demand expands.

Industrial relations

The early 1980s has seen attempts by government to intervene in industrial relations through the legal process. In the US air traffic controllers were dismissed en masse during their strike in 1982, when the Federal Government declared that they were breaking the law. The strike leaders were arrested and the union collapsed. In the UK, the 1980 and 1982 Employment Acts restricted trade union immunities from legal action by employers, outlawed sympathetic strikes, secondary picketing, and introduced heavy penalties against employers and unions where an individual was dismissed for refusing to join a closed shop. Legislation has been introduced which is aimed at making secret ballots compulsory prior to strike action, and at curtailing the financial links between trade unions and the Labour Party. EEC-sponsored changes are also in prospect, such as the Fifth Directive on employee participation.

From the perspective of personnel management, the law in industrial relations seems here to stay. Legal intervention is not necessarily welcome, but following the extension of rights to individuals through various forms of protection against unfair dismissal, health and safety legislation and compensation for redundancy in the 1960s and 1970s throughout Europe, it was inevitable that some attempt should be made to regulate the affairs of trade unions and employers by statute. For the personnel manager, the minefield of injunctions and court cases arising from the NGA and Stockport Messenger dispute will be a salutary lesson. Most personnel people will want to avoid tangles of that sort, and thus we may see a return to the emphasis on proper procedures, which will prevent such overt conflict.

Trade unions in the UK are faced with a large-scale reduction in membership, and are under financial pressures to make changes.[14] With falling membership and rising costs, and higher benefits expenditure, there will be a number of changes to trade unions in the years ahead. Some trade unions, such as the Transport and General Workers' Union are in a healthier position than others, but we may expect mergers, with larger more viable unions to emerge. The numbers of trade unions have fallen in the last 20 years from 650 to about 400, while more people have joined the larger unions in that time.

One way out of the difficulties would be for the unions to appoint more professional management, especially in the investment and husbandry of their resources. The benefits they offer will need to be more closely tailored to modern requirements, and sold to a sceptical, price conscious membership. This may result in new forms of collective bargaining, featuring longer-term agreements over wider issues. Some more politically motivated members could interpret these developments as the incorporation of trade unions into management, at a time when traditional political alliances are being questioned.

So far we have described some of the likely areas where changes will continue to affect the personnel role. There are links between these movements. There is an affinity between more employee involvement in decision-making, and the broad social trend towards a greater awareness by companies of ecological and health issues. These seem to be complementary drives for reform, with the objectives of making managements more accountable to a wider constituency. In addition to broad 'societal' level change, there are a number of different levels at which change is likely to influence our lives.

The range of variables which is influencing our lives means a fast pace for change, and a considerable amount of change. With so many different influences on the personnel specialist, the future should bring more choice about how to perform the role: about what kind of personnel model to create.

Future personnel policies

How should the personnel function respond to these changes in society? How will personnel management develop as the specialist occupation reaches its centenary? What new initiatives might we expect from the personnel function?

Human resource planning
Given that some attempts at the integration of personnel policies have been made, we would see the appropriate responses to the changes in our economy and society coming from senior management as a whole. The personnel function is enhanced by its involvement in formal strategic planning. These corporate planning routines are now well established in large UK companies, and have been adapted for use by larger Japanese, United States, European and multinational corporations for some time. As we progress to the end of the century, it seems likely that corporate planning will be more acceptable to smaller organizations. Paradoxically, the recession has pointed to the need for planning a business strategy, and as costs increase, a recognition of the people part of the strategy has come to many managers who previously lived for the here and now, without a thought for costs or long-term profitability.

The personnel policy outcomes from these strategic plans are in each of the main personnel areas. These will be assessed in relation to their costs, and the impact on the performance measures selected (such as added value, or return on capital invested). Thus we expect to see personnel objectives expressed as financial contributions to the business.

Employee relations

The old industrial relations game is dead. We now play by different rules, and this difference is accentuated by the use of the term *employee* relations rather than industrial relations. Future personnel management is likely to be less concerned with the old institutional framework of trade unions, and more involved with managing the employment relationship as a whole at a strategic level. Recently the trend has been towards bargaining at the company or unit level, according to the strategy adopted by the organization. The move away from traditional industrial relations, away from the district or national level, means de facto company unions in many cases. There is now more power in the hands of the employer, with the unemployment weapon, and 'give back' bargaining has emerged where flexibility, reduced manning and an element of deskilling has been taking place. Deskilling could be termed multi-skilling if one accepts that the skills are not acquired with the same degree of depth as previously.

Shop stewards are still important at the local level. The stress on changing working practices has, if anything, enhanced the role of the workplace representative and, as part of their change tactics, companies are becoming more interested in devising productive forms of employee involvement. Quality circles are one manifestation of a worldwide movement to improve the quality of goods and services by drawing on existing employee know-how to solve work problems. Although originating in Japan, the idea has now been translated into many different formats according to traditions and cultures. By January 1981 there were estimated to be 40 British companies with quality circles, by 1983 there were over 200.[15]

The agreements reached with Japanese companies operating in the UK, with one trade union representing the whole workforce, pendulum arbitration, tough rules on discipline and common status show that it is possible to achieve a new approach to industrial relations in the UK. There is also evidence that some trade union officials welcome the clarity and consistency which such an approach brings.[16]

Reward structures

There has been a growth in the number of arrangements to harmonize pay between monthly-paid and hourly-rated people, although this can be a particularly expensive policy change if pensions are to be included in the new rewards package. The equal value provision might give rise to more job evaluation exercises, in addition to growth caused by rationalization of pay policies. Managerial salaries are more likely to contain a variable element, with the trend being towards long-term incentives which relate to long-term performance, and include participative elements, such as stock option schemes, encouraged by the present Government through tax concessions. Flexible benefit policies are operated only by a small number of companies at present, but we might anticipate an element of choice about benefits.[17]

Recruitment and training
As personnel policies become more integrated, so it is more difficult to identify individual policies. This means that in recruitment the crucial determinant of success is seen to be how the new recruit will adapt to the present and future requirements of the organization. Trainability testing, group selection methods and an increased use of psychometric tests reflect this emphasis. The availability of labour has shifted recruitment policy towards finding people who can make a contribution, and who will be effective quickly, whose personal style fits the company culture, and who are adaptable to future change, hence a desire to recruit staff who are intelligent, since this is a good predictor of adaptability, as intelligence reflects the capacity and speed of learning.[18]

A flexible approach towards employment contracts, with more part-time and sub-contracting may bring the need for new personnel skills. Personnel staff will need to become expert in how to handle and how to induct consultants, and be able to present the recruitment policy in the same 'make or buy-in' terms already used by their marketing and financial colleagues. More women in the labour force will highlight dual career problems. Restricted promotion opportunities may result in a plateau being reached at an early stage in a person's career. There are problems of executive 'burn-out', of stress caused by the pace of change amongst more junior employees, and the diagnosis of those stress-related illnesses which cause problems will become more important. This catalogue of issues is a partial agenda for the recruitment and training policies of the future to handle. A greater awareness of employment costs could also lead to a rapid reappraisal of recruitment policy. The changes to national insurance contributions announced in the 1984 Budget will cost ICI about £4 million for example.

There will no doubt be a variety of responses from organizations to these changes. We might anticipate a more effective lobby on governments in order to help cope with the changes, for example to persuade the government to clarify the self-employed status, and to be more consistent in its policies which affect the costs of employment.

In the training field, the Government's aim seems to be to produce a workforce with basic general skills on to which the more advanced or job-specific knowledge can be bolted. This is potentially a good way of overcoming skill shortages, but the diminishing number of formal apprenticeships, and the abolition of most Training Boards puts the responsibility back to the employers for creating coherent training policies. A growth area for personnel specialists is in designing more sophisticated methods of analysing training needs. Here we would see the social sciences playing an increasingly important part and, with the related issue of training evaluation, we would anticipate more organizational resources to be made available for this task, whatever model of personnel management is adopted. This we believe will go together with developments in distance learning using computer-based methods, and interactive videos where feedback to the trainee is instant, and the training can be monitored continually. Many companies have already invested in distance learning, (such as the retail banks, and many large companies – Thorn EMI, Wimpey for example). Distance learning university courses are also on the market, following the pioneering work of the Open University.

Management development has grown in significance, not only as a way of developing key skills in managers, to make the company more competitive, but also as a method of changing the organization, by introducing a common management philosophy. Good examples here are the Granada Group, Jaguar Cars, May and Baker British Shipbuilders, and in smaller companies such as Richard Clay plc (a small printer). The old notions of management development in many corporations have been replaced by ideas of manager development – through job enlargement, mentoring and coaching. For those personnel specialists who are involved, management development work offers a chance to influence the style of management and the strategic development of their organizations. If the 1960s was an era for the industrial relations specialist, the 1980s is the period of the management development expert.

Human resources management
As a conclusion, we wish to summarize briefly the way the personnel role is changing, as a consequence of the developments we have outlined. The personnel response through the management team will take on the more credible status of a necessary management activity, as we have stressed in Chapters 6 and 7, as a result of integrating measurable objectives for personnel policies. Increased emphasis on strategic planning will highlight the way cultural and social factors influence the future of business. We would see the need for personnel specialists to bring these wider issues into decision-making. Business strategy is not totally encompassed by the formal corporate planning procedures. Strategy can also be seen as an emergent series of actions, where flexibility and accurate prediction are essential. Decision-making requires a choice between options, and therefore the evaluation of alternatives. To make a worthwhile contribution, the personnel specialists will have to rely on knowledge and research from the social sciences and, we would suggest, on data

processing to analyse the information available on record.

There is a major role for the personnel specialist in the implementation stage. Managing the change process requires a coherence of approach and a sensitivity to the people, the issues and institutions involved, which is the hallmark of the competent personnel specialist. The management of communications, and the implementation of a common management style and philosophy, have produced major benefits for companies at the leading edge of personnel work. The personnel role in support of the business strategy takes the business over the difficult hurdle of the implementation of the strategy.

The personnel role in the future will also require the initiation of major moves forward. Personnel departments in the more advanced companies will be expected to propose changes which will gain productivity improvements. Quality of working life campaigns, as part of a 'hearts and minds' exercise may be introduced with the aim of reducing tensions, increasing employee involvement and releasing energy. In broad terms, these exercises help to gain acceptance of organizational belief systems. Moves to build effective teams by exercises, group work, selection using team roles as criteria for acceptance, and feedback on interpersonal perceptions are likely to become more common, as the costs of unproductive relationships are revealed. Similarly, the harmonization of payment systems, flexible benefit packages and radical moves on longer-term agreement with trade unions are initiatives which will become increasingly appropriate as mechanisms for pushing organizations into the twenty-first century.

We expect changes to the personnel role in two ways over the next decade. Experts in very specific aspects of managing the employment relationship are likely to blossom, beyond even the current multiplicity of managers with titles such as 'compensation manager', or 'recruitment manager'. Experts in compensation will need to be specialists in the tax effectiveness of benefits, and to be able to cope with tailor-made job evaluation schemes, to handle post-harmonization problems for example. We have already commented on the growing significance of management development. Similarly, communication experts, and public relations experts are needed more to coordinate the internal and external image of the company. The second way in which the role will develop, we believe, will be through the 'business manager' route, where there is an 'architect' model of personnel work. We see this as going beyond internal management, with more external roles for the 'architect' personnel manager, who will be required to network more, to be a resource investigator commissioning consultants, become more involved in difficult ethical issues, such as those raised by the societal roles of personnel, or where assessment data is used and passed on to other managers.

From this bifurcation, between expert, internal consultant, and business manager, operating in the 'architect' mode there is a question of what will happen to the personnel generalist? It seems likely that those whose functions have been largely administrative, whose work is easily computerized, are most vulnerable. There is still a place for each of the models we have described. Each has the possibility of redefinition as an expert or a 'business manager'. The future we believe will bring a new breed of 'business managers' deploying the human resources of the company. The increasingly used term 'human resource management' seems to foretell the advent of this shift. New technology is driving this shift as much as economic pressures.

Organizations whose implicit direction (if not announced intent), creates a personnel function which corresponds to our clerk of works or contracts manager paradigms, is no less entitled to demand efficient automated systems on the part of the professionals. Rightly, senior management should demand current and accurate record-keeping, efficient and cost-effective recruitment administration, effective salary administration and so on. Indeed, the extension of automation in the personnel function, in the UK at least, seems to be going in the direction of increasing administration applications as significantly as introducing advanced planning applications.

The Institute of Manpower Studies' survey of computers in personnel reported on the situation in over 500 companies.[19] The anticipated developments in 1984 and 1985 are foreseen in such areas as recruitment administration, absence control, development and training, manpower budget administration and contract administration.

The advanced planning applications which are foreseen as being required beyond 1984, include manpower number forecasting, integrated manpower budgeting, management accounting and manpower cost forecasting. The range of applications is narrower and, significantly, the existing applications in these areas in 1982 and 1983 were dramatically fewer. Of the respondents, for example, 29% already had recruitment administration systems, only 11% had manpower cost forecasting models; 27% had manpower budgeting systems and 14% had applications which integrated labour costs derived from personnel databases and the organization's management accounting system.

There is a significant place therefore for the automated office in support of clerk of works and contracts manager models of personnel management. Conferences and exhibitions in recent years have provided the opportunities to demonstrate the pervasive role automation has in the personnel function. But office automation – the application of predominantly electronic technologies to office work – is one thing, information technology another.

Human resources management – essential in the architect's view of personnel management – needs information technology and information management to function at all. Information technology now inhabits all areas of organizational life including personnel management. Information technology – a broader concept than office automation – will support human resource management but what is human resource management? Is it a more elegant or fashionable way of saying 'personnel management is that part of management concerned with people at work and with their relationships with an organization?' Is human resource management a 'rose by any other name', or is it a more fundamental redefinition of personnel management? If the answer is in the affirmative, then we can be satisfied that the architect model of personnel management is qualitatively different from our clerk of works and contracts managers models.

We are not going to provide an encapsulating and tidy definition. Human resource management as an alternative view to traditional personnel management, as much as any other issue, involves a changed perception of the individual at work and the employment relationship.

Our traditional thinking is conditioned by the simple dictum of the economic sages: the factors of production are labour, land and capital. All three have a physical existence; they are tangible resources capable of employment (or of being left unemployed) for the purpose of the enterprise. In short, employees are a purchased service – undoubtedly to be treated well either because their good treatment will maximize their output or perhaps because the organization considers their good treatment to be morally correct. Social history suggests the reason has more to do with state intervention and the imposition of minimum standards in many aspects of the master and servant contract than any moral imperatives. Notwithstanding the quality of work life – and who is to say that in historical terms it has not improved radically with the early welfare tradition in management playing its part – labour still remains a factor of production.

A human resources management philosophy comes about in an organization when this view diminishes and disappears to be replaced with the perception that labour is not an expense of doing business, but that people are the only resource capable of turning inanimate factors of production into wealth. People provide the source of creative energy in any direction the organization dictates and fosters.

The increase in technology in its various guises in all enterprises provides the architect with opportunities not with a diminished role. Ultimately, technology becomes 'stalemated' among competing enterprises and the competitive edge lies in the creative use of talent and the optimum design and organization of work to provide personal motivation. Material rewards for those in work can go well beyond the satisfaction of basic needs; working for economic surplus or personal fulfillment can be the drives. In high value-added enterprises, the edge resides in the brainpower of people, not the robotics of manufacture, assembly or delivering of a service. Human resource management is a more comprehensive approach to the organization of people at work.

With a base in the behavioural sciences, human resource management is concerned about the motivation and development of the individual employee and the performance and productivity of the organization. The distinction between this position and the traditional view of personnel management is perhaps not too great. But where the rupture has come, where the architect model is distinguishable from the contracts manager and most certainly the clerk of works, the personnel function has been redefined and expanded from the role of being a control-oriented supplier of labour to an overall human resource planning, development and utilization agency.

It goes beyond the classical personnel management position and has as its starting point the integration and coordination of people planning with overall strategy formulation and corporate planning. The personnel professional operating in this mode can earn a coequal place in the inner circle of decision-takers. He or she will become the manager of a system which recognizes the interdependence of technology, markets, capital, organization structure, job design and individual personal goals and motivation.

Human resource management is a holistic view wherein all activities are designed in a unified, interlocking manner, not a series of unrelated events. Classical personnel management has not been granted a position in decision-taking circles because it has frequently not earned one. It has not been concerned with the totality of the organization but often with issues which have been not only parochial but esoteric to boot. What ties human resource management together is a belief in the potential value and productive contribution of the individual. Personnel management in an architect mode is directed at achieving the symbiosis which is seen to exist between the organization and its goals and an effective use of the human resources the organization needs to achieve those goals.

Notes

1 A. Toffler, *Future Shock* (London: Bodley-Head, 1970).
   D. Bell, *The Coming of Post-Industrial Society* (London: Heinemann, 1974).
   C. Jenkins and B. Sherman, *The Collapse of Work* (Eyre Methuen, 1979).
2 J. Naisbitt, *Megatrends: 10 new directions transforming our lives* (London: MacDonald and Co., 1984).
3 *The Department of Employment Gazette* publishes monthly statistics on the labour market. In December 1984, the national average unemployment rate of 13% masked regional variations from 21% in Northern Ireland, 18% in the North of England, and 15% in Wales and in the West Midlands of England.
4 D.H. Freeman (ed.), *Employment Outlook and Insights* (Geneva: ILO, 1979).
5 'France: A series of measures on employment flexibility', *European Industrial Relations Review* (May 1985), p. 12.
6 *Lifting the Burden*. White Paper (HMSO, 1985).
7 'Office automation, personnel and the new technology', *Personnel Journal* (October 1980).
   'The automated office', *Management Today* special survey (April 1982).
8 C. Handy, *The Future of Work* (Oxford: Basil Blackwell, 1984).
   See also C. Brewster and S. Connock, *Industrial Relations: Cost Effective Strategies* (London: Hutchinson, 1985).
9 A. Toffler, *The Third Wave* (London: Collins, 1980).

10 T. Burns and G.M. Stalker, *The Management of Innovation* (London: Tavistock, 1961).

11 R. Heller, 'British business profitability league', *Management Today* (October, 1983).

12 'Growth in holidays with pay and in reduction of hours', *Employment Gazette* (April 1985), pp. 154–6.

13 'Recent trends in labour costs', *Employment Gazette* (March 1984).

14 *Annual Reports of Certification Officer*. 1978, 1979, 1980, 1981, 1983, 1984. Crown Copyright. (Certification Office for Trade Unions and Employers' Associations).

15 J. Bank and B. Wilpert, 'What's so special about quality circles?', *Journal of General Management*, vol. 9, no. 1 (Autumn 1983).

16 D.W. Bevan, 'Japanese management in Britain: a union to the defence', *Journal of the Institute of Supervisory Management*, vol. 36, no. 2 (Summer 1985).

17 K.R. Allen, 'Compensating for the future', *Benefits International* (January 1984).

18 G. Jessup and H. Jessup, *Selection and Assessment at Work* (London: Methuen, 1975).

19 *Computers in Personnel Management Survey* (Institute of Manpower Studies, 1983).

Index